African and Oceanic Art in Jerusalem

African and Oceanic Art in Jerusalem
The Israel Museum Collection

Douglas Newton

 The Israel Museum, Jerusalem

The Israel Museum, Jerusalem

African and Oceanic Art in Jerusalem
The Israel Museum Collection
by Douglas Newton

Acting Curator, Arts of Africa, Oceania,
and the Americas: Martin Wright
Associate Curator, Arts of Africa
and Oceania: Dorit Shafir

Design: Yael Bamberger
Editing: Stacey Brooks
Supplemental editing: Vivian Oppenheim, Anna Barber
Photographs © The Israel Museum, Jerusalem
by Meidad Suchowolski
Illustrations © The Israel Museum, Jerusalem
by Pnina Arad
Color separations: Shapiro Repro Ltd., Tel Aviv
Printing: Art Plus Ltd., Jerusalem

Catalogue no. 448
ISBN 965 278 262 9

On the cover: Reliquary figure (*boho na bwete*)
Gabon: Hongwe, late 19th – early 20th century

The publication was made possible by
The Maremont Foundation
The Weiss Fund
Ellen and Jerome Stern
The Faith-dorian and Martin Wright Family Fund
The Solow Foundation

Contents

Foreword

The Israel Museum was conceived as a national museum – emphasizing the archaeology of ancient Israel and the arts of modern Israel and of Jewish cultures worldwide, but also representing the great cultures of the modern world. Its founders in 1965 therefore envisioned an encyclopedic museum, comparable with the other great national museums of the world which are fully international in scope.

This concept was the impetus for the early development of the Museum's collections of what used to be called "primitive art," beginning with the opening in 1979 of the Arnold Maremont Gallery for Precolumbian Art, through the generosity of the collectors Arnold and Eileen Maremont of Chicago and through the Maremont Foundation, which has sustained its tradition of support since Arnold Maremont's death. As early as 1976, Martin and Faith-dorian Wright of New York had pledged generously to establish galleries for Oceanic, African, and North American Indian Art, realizing this commitment with the opening of the Galleries for Art from North America and Oceania in 1981, followed by the Gallery for African Art in 1984. The opening of the African Art Gallery was celebrated with an international symposium on the arts of preliterate societies, under the distinguished chairmanship of Claude Lévi-Strauss. Finally, in 1986, Benjamin Weiss of New York provided a substantial endowment to assure the appropriate museological development of these collections and of the department that would preserve and maintain them. In this way, the Department for the Arts of Africa, Oceania, and the Americas was, in a notably short time, established and solidly secured.

With this framework in place, the department and its collections continued to flourish, thanks to the involvement of many patrons. It has been the consistent and grateful beneficiary of the generosity of many great collectors, among them: Alex Antebi, New York; Lisa Bradley, New York; Sam Dubiner, Ramat Gan; Marc and Denyse Ginzberg, Rye, NY; Arne and Milly Glimcher, New York; Jay and Jean Kislak, Miami; Cedric and Daisy Marks, New York; Edward M. and Vivian Merrin, New York; Carl T. Shipman, Toorak, Australia; and Jerome and Ellen Stern, New York. Most recently, the department benefited from a substantial bequest from the Arthur and Madeleine Chalette Lejwa Collection, New York, and an important gift of African art from Lawrence Gussman of Scarsdale, NY.

The Museum's Galleries for the Arts of Africa, Oceania, and the Americas now boast a remarkably rich presentation of outstanding works – unique for our geographic position in the world and central to the realization of our founders' dream that the Israel Museum become a leading repository of world culture. In this regard, the present time seems very appropriate for the presentation of this publication, documenting a collection which is already well-known to experts in the field, but which deserves to be even better known to a broadly interested public worldwide. For the scholarship that it contains, we are most deeply grateful to two international authorities, Douglas Newton and Kate Ezra, and for the quality and variety of the works featured, we are indebted to the collectors and patrons whose exemplary generosity is documented herein.

This publication benefited from the creativity and hard work of many members of the Museum's staff, coordinated by Dorit Shafir, Associate Curator of the Arts of Africa and Oceania. Our greatest thanks nonetheless must be reserved for Faith-dorian and Martin Wright, as we salute the unique combination of Martin's roles as Museum professional, patron, and adviser. His exemplary dedication and his tireless work on the Museum's behalf have been instrumental in the blossoming of a truly remarkable department and collection, which have become a source of greatest pride to the Israel Museum.

James S. Snyder
Anne and Jerome Fisher Director

Douglas Newton, senior adviser to the Israel Museum's Department for the Arts of Africa, Oceania, and the Americas since its inception, died on September 19, 2001, shortly after approving the final proofs of this book for printing. He had devoted several years to the writing of its text, and during that time he generously contributed objects from his own collection in order to fill certain gaps in our holdings.

A world authority on the art of the Pacific Islands, Douglas Newton also played a unique role in bringing so-called primitive art to the attention of museum-goers. He organized and designed dozens of ground-breaking exhibitions and oversaw the creation of the Metropolitan Museum's Michael C. Rockefeller Wing, in which the arts of Africa, Oceania, and the Americas achieved unprecedented prominence in a general museological setting.

Truly a scholar and a gentleman, Douglas was a close personal friend and a steadfast friend of the Israel Museum. It is with great sadness that we dedicate this volume to his memory.

M. W.

Preface

In 1963 my wife and I first began to collect the artwork of the fascinating cultures of Africa and Oceania. Faith-dorian had studied art at New York University in the 1950s, when NYU was the home of the New York school of abstract expressionism. Her teachers included the well-known African-American painter Hale Woldruffe, who owned a group of African sculptures that first made her aware of this beautiful and complex art. After our marriage in 1955, she introduced me to the field, and we ourselves were inspired to start a collection. When we became committed to supporting the growth of the Israel Museum, it was Faith-dorian's wish to do so as a memorial to her father, Abraham Janoff, an ardent Zionist. For this reason, much of the collection we have given to the Museum has been presented in his memory.

Over the years we have witnessed the rapid growth of the Department for the Arts of Africa, Oceania, and the Americas, which would not have been possible without the outstanding generosity of our donors around the world, the active involvement of the Museum's directors and curators, and the valued guidance of experts in the field. From the very start, Martin Weyl, Chief Curator and later Director of the Museum, provided the wholehearted support necessary to bring our plans to fruition, as have the present Director, James Snyder, Chief Curator-at-Large Yigal Zalmona, and Chief Curator of the Arts Suzanne Landau. Our friend Douglas Newton, formerly of New York's Museum of Primitive Art and the Metropolitan Museum, and now our senior adviser, has been of immense help from the outset, and has also devoted much time to the preparation of the present volume. Two other advisers have played important roles: Kate Ezra – formerly of the Metropolitan Museum – in African art, and Edward M. Merrin, who provided counsel in the area of Precolumbian art. In recent years, the department has benefited greatly from the dedicated efforts of Yvonne Fleitman, Associate Curator of Art of the Americas, and Dorit Shafir, Associate Curator of Arts of Africa and Oceania, who also deserves our thanks for her part in the creation of this book.

Faith-dorian and I have derived great satisfaction from our role in the development of this wonderful cultural monument, and it is our hope that, in the years to come, the Israel Museum will continue to bring the great arts of the world to a growing domestic and international public.

Martin Wright
Acting Curator, Arts of Africa, Oceania, and the Americas

Acknowledgments

I am indebted to all those who have worked with me on the preparation of this book, and it is a privilege to name them here.

My gratitude to those members of the Israel Museum whose warm welcome has made my work so personally enjoyable: Martin Weyl, former Director of the Israel Museum, who initiated the project, and Yigal Zalmona, Chief Curator-at-Large. James Snyder, present Director, has been unfailingly supportive throughout. Current and past members of the Department, Timna Seligman, Yvonne Fleitman, and Dorit Shafir – under whose wing the African and Oceanic collections are cared for – have contributed a great deal. Their steadfast help, enthusiasm, and cooperation have been a constant pleasure over the several years during which the collections, and this book, have grown.

Dr. Kate Ezra, my friend and former colleague at the Metropolitan Museum of Art in New York, some years ago made a perceptive selection of African works that afforded me significant guidance. Since then she has reviewed my texts and choices of African objects to their great benefit, in the generous spirit she has shown so often before, and contributes a valuable introduction to them.

Sincere thanks are due to Virginia-Lee Webb and Ross Day, of the Goldwater Library of the Metropolitan Museum of Art and its Photograph Collection, for their help with research materials.

I am grateful to Stacey Brooks and Vivian Oppenheim, my indefatigable editors, for saving me from grammatical solecisms, and either clarifying my texts or inciting me to do so.

Faith-dorian and Martin Wright have been my close friends for many years. To their dedication and scholarly interest, to their advocacy and generosity with their time, efforts, and gifts, are due the existence and progress of the collection. They have been, and continue to be, its architects. They brought me the happy opportunity to work with it: for this and much else I offer them my deepest thanks, and I dedicate my part in this book to them.

Douglas Newton

Acknowledgments

The success of a book such as this is dependent on the labor and talent of many people from various fields of endeavor, who invested much time and effort in its preparation. Having been given the task of acting as liaison among them all, I am very pleased to have the opportunity to thank the individuals who were instrumental in bringing this project to fruition.

Much gratitude is due to the staff of the Israel Museum's Publications Department under the expert guidance of Nirit Zur, in particular to editors Vivian Oppenheim and Anna Barber and to Yael Bamberger, whose good taste and love of the objects is reflected in the book's design. We are also indebted to Meidad Suchowolski, whose creativity resulted in exquisite photographs, to photographer Avshalom Avital, who came to the rescue with solutions for seemingly insoluble problems, and to Pnina Arad, who prepared the line drawings. Sylvia Pinhassy of the Art Wing provided secretarial assistance, and Nechama Margulies was responsible for typesetting.

For their involvement with the objects themselves — the raison d'être of the department and this publication — many thanks to: Ruhi Baharad, Marina Rassovsky, and Irit Lev of the Museum's laboratories; Moris Lasry and Menahem Amin of the Technical Services Department headed by Pesach Ruder; art handlers Artur Avakov and Dan Divinsky; and Shana Kaplan, Monique Birenbaum, and Arlene Bodner of the American Friends of the Israel Museum. Finally, thanks are due to the Israel Museum's Registrar, Miriam Apfeldorf, and her assistant Bareket Mann, and to the staff of the Shipping Department: Daphna Lapidot, Henk van Doornik, Tal Eliaspur, Tali Kopfstein, and Aviva Kat.

Dorit Shafir
Associate Curator, Arts of Africa and Oceania

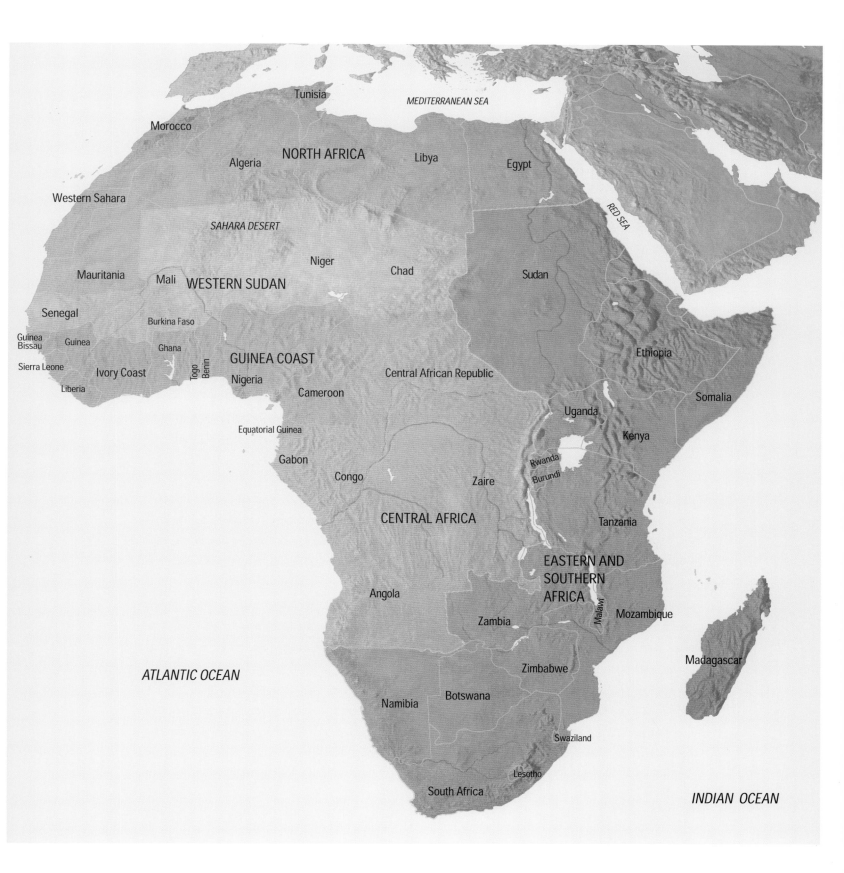

Tunisia

MEDITERRANEAN SEA

Morocco

NORTH AFRICA

Algeria

Libya

Egypt

Western Sahara

RED SEA

SAHARA DESERT

Niger

Chad

Sudan

Mauritania

Mali

WESTERN SUDAN

Senegal

Burkina Faso

Ethiopia

Guinea
Bissau

Guinea

Ghana

GUINEA COAST

Somalia

Sierra Leone

Togo
Benin

Ivory Coast

Nigeria

Central African Republic

Liberia

Cameroon

Uganda

Equatorial Guinea

Kenya

Gabon

Rwanda

Congo

Burundi

Zaire

CENTRAL AFRICA

Tanzania

EASTERN AND
SOUTHERN
AFRICA

Angola

Malawi

Mozambique

Zambia

ATLANTIC OCEAN

Zimbabwe

Madagascar

Namibia

Botswana

Swaziland

Lesotho

South Africa

INDIAN OCEAN

Africa

Introduction

The arts of Africa are diverse and complex. The continent is home to more than 850 million people who belong to over a thousand different ethnic groups, each with its own language, culture, and artistic traditions. In Africa today many people live in villages according to patterns established hundreds – if not thousands – of years ago. At the same time, millions of their compatriots live in huge modern cities that are more like New York, London, or Tel Aviv.

Africa has produced some of the world's oldest surviving works of art and some of the most exciting contemporary works as well. The scope of Africa's rich artistic heritage is evident in this catalogue of highlights of the Israel Museum collection. The collection focuses on the sculptural traditions of African peoples living south of the Sahara Desert. There are, of course, many African art forms besides sculpture, such as pottery, metalwork, architecture, textiles, dress, and body arts, but these are not fully examined here. Also not included are the contemporary arts produced by both academically trained artists and others adapting and exploring the new materials, subjects, and conditions presented by the modern and postmodern world. Instead, the Israel Museum's collection concentrates on what some call "classical" African art. These are art forms that relate to cultural practices whose roots extend back prior to the nineteenth and twentieth centuries – before intensified contact with European culture brought about dramatic changes in African society.

The Setting

Within these "classical" traditions, there is much variety, reflecting the diverse geographic regions south of the Sahara. The continent's climate and vegetation zones are roughly symmetrical on either side of the equator, changing from the tropical rain forest along the equator to progressively drier areas to the north and south, and culminating in the Sahara and Kalahari Deserts.

South of the Sahara is an area of grassy plains covered with scattered trees known as savanna, where rainfall is sparse and concentrated into a single rainy season lasting half the year. The western part of this geographic area, known as the Western Sudan, is an important art-producing area and includes the modern countries of Mali, Burkina Faso, and the northern parts of Guinea, Côte d'Ivoire, Ghana, Togo, Benin, and Nigeria.

To the south are the forest zones, characterized by dense trees and plentiful rainfall throughout the year. The area usually referred to as the Guinea Coast hugs the shore of West Africa from Senegal to Nigeria. Central Africa can also be divided into a forest region – which stretches along the equator from Cameroon across northern Congo to the great lakes – and a savanna region parallel to it but further south. East Africa and South Africa have distinct, drier environments, inhabited by nomadic herdsmen.

Most of the art featured in this volume originated in the forest and savanna areas of West and Central Africa, which supported settled agricultural populations with the natural and cultural resources to create permanent works of art. The art traditions of East and South Africa are rich in portable, decorated, utilitarian objects of wood, pottery, hide, and beadwork, but these are not included here.

History

Most African sculpture is made of wood, a plentiful material in the forest and savanna regions. This poses certain problems for the study of African art, since wood has a limited life span in a tropical environment. It is unlikely that African sculpture made of wood or other organic materials can survive more than one or two hundred years. Thus, art historians must look to other types of objects to gain a historical perspective on African art.

The most important resources of this kind are works of art in more durable materials such as terra-cotta, iron, copper alloys, and stone. These works, such as the Nok terra-cotta figure made 2,500 years ago (p. 81), provide valuable information about the development of African art. Moreover, they have the added advantage of yielding accurate dating information through scientific testing of their materials or of their archaeological contexts. Where known, these dates are included in the catalogue. In the vast majority of cases of African wood sculpture, however, precise dating is not possible – although it can be assumed that most examples included here were made between the mid-nineteenth and the mid-twentieth century.

A complete history of African art remains to be written, although we know that its origins extend back as far as human beings have engaged in representing their world. The earliest known works of art from the African continent are the paintings on rocks found in the Apollo 11 shelter in southern Namibia, which were made between 27,500 and 25,500 years ago. This makes them as old, if not older, than much of the Paleolithic art of western Europe, such as the cave paintings of Lascaux or Altamira – and proves that Africans invented their own art independent of outside influence.

Rock paintings and engravings are found in many sites throughout Africa. The largest concentration of them were made in the mountains of the central Sahara (in the southern part of present-day Algeria), beginning about 8000 BCE, when this area was lush and well-watered. The Sahara was then home to abundant animal, fish, and plant life, as well as to human communities of hunters and gatherers, all of which are represented in the paintings.

Over the next few thousand years the climate gradually became drier, the flora and fauna changed, and the peoples of the Sahara learned to herd animals and cultivate crops, again illustrated in their paintings. By the third millennium BCE, the continued drying of the Sahara forced people to move to more hospitable areas and to settle in permanent agricultural communities. Some may have migrated to ancient Egypt, while others found their way to the savannas of sub-Saharan Africa.

The earliest known sculptures from sub-Saharan Africa come from the Nok culture mentioned earlier, located in present-day northern Nigeria. The Nok people were farmers who also smelted iron, which they used to make hoes and other tools. The Nok sculptures, which date from about 500 BCE to 200 CE, have much in common with later works of African art. They represent the human form through geometric abstractions of facial features and body parts, and they alter the natural proportions of the body to give prominence to the head. In addition, these works reproduce in great detail the elaborate coiffures and beaded body ornaments with which the Nok individuals distinguished themselves; these elements continue to feature in the dress of later African peoples and their sculpted representations of themselves.

During the first millennium CE, several powerful and wealthy states arose in the savanna and forest areas of West Africa, from which fascinating works of art have survived. The Ghana and Mali empires, established in the eighth and thirteenth centuries, respectively, thrived by trading gold northwards across the Sahara. In exchange, they received life-sustaining commodities such as salt, as well as other materials that had a direct impact on works of art, such as copper, beads, and textiles. The city of Jenne-Jeno, located in the inland delta region of the Niger River, at the juncture between the desert and savanna, was an important stop along the trans-Saharan trade routes; it is thought to be the earliest city in West Africa. Terra-cotta sculptures, such as the one on p. 27, have been found in Jenne-Jeno and its surrounding area, dating from about 1000 to 1300 CE.

Jenne-Jeno and other centers in the savanna region of West Africa were part of a vast trading network that stretched north across the Sahara and south into the forests along the coast, as evidenced by works of art found in sites like Ife, in southwestern Nigeria. By the beginning of the second millennium, this city was the center of a wealthy and powerful kingdom; to this day, it maintains its status as the spiritual capital of the Yoruba people.

Ife's artists created sculpture whose pronounced naturalism sets it apart from most other African art, past and present. Most of these sensitively modeled and idealized sculptures were made of terra-cotta, like the example on p. 83. Others were made of imported copper and brass, demonstrating Ife's trade links to the wider world. The sculptures from Ife were made between the twelfth and fifteenth century, after which time the nearby city of Benin replaced Ife as a political, economic, and artistic center.

Benin was the capital of a vast and powerful kingdom whose divine king and numerous court officials were represented in thousands of works of art in brass and ivory (among them, the plaque pendant seen on p. 85). The history of Benin encapsulates much of the African continent's relationship with Europeans since the mid-fifteenth century, when European navigators first ventured along the coast of West Africa. Quick to establish trading partnerships that were mutually beneficial, these early traders exchanged iron, copper, textiles, and guns for gold, ivory, spices, and – tragically – slaves.

For the next hundred years, European contacts with Africa were largely limited to the coastal areas. By the nineteenth century, however, explorers and missionaries had begun to probe the interior of the continent in search of both natural resources to fuel

Europe's industrial revolution and human souls to convert to Christianity. In the "scramble for Africa" at the end of the nineteenth century, wars of conquest such as Britain's 1897 Benin Punitive Expedition effectively divided the continent into colonies ruled by European powers.

Ironically, the thousands of royal objects seized by the British in Benin were instrumental in changing European perceptions about African art. When the objects were brought to England and sold, the museum curators and private collectors who bought them were stunned by the technical virtuosity and refined naturalism of these lost-wax castings and delicate ivory carvings. For the first time, comparisons were made between African art pieces and masterworks of European art. Not long afterward, in the first decade of the twentieth century, avant-garde artists such as Picasso, Braque, and Matisse in France and Kirchner, Nolde, and Pechstein in Germany discovered affinities between their own artwork and the African sculptures and masks they saw in the ethnographic museums recently established in the major cities of the colonial powers. The geometric abstraction, altered anatomy, and bold colors of the African sculptures validated and reinforced the European artists' own experiments, contributing to the development of Cubism, Fauvism, German Expressionism, and other modern art movements. This enthusiasm eventually led to a more widespread interest in — and acceptance of — the African objects as works of art rather than mere artifacts of material culture.

During the colonial period, colonial government policies, Christian missionaries, and new forms of education, employment, and even health care often undermined — intentionally or unintentionally — the structures of political, economic, religious, and family life that had been the traditional context for creating and using art. More often than not, art forms and the cultural practices that gave rise to them adapted to the new circumstances. Artists began to use newly available materials — such as oil-based enamel paints — and newly observed imagery, such as Western-style clothing and automobiles. Masquerades were performed for newly created circumstances, such as visits of colonial officers or European holidays. Although these changes often demonstrate the vitality and resilience of African art, many museums and collectors intentionally avoid objects that reflect such innovations, instead emphasizing works that suggest a pristine, unchanging past.

Following World War II, Africans' desire to liberate themselves from colonial rule intensified, and by 1960 most European colonies in Africa had become independent nations ruled by Africans. The second half of the twentieth century has seen major changes in the way art is produced in Africa. Beginning in the colonial period and increasing after independence, European-style art schools or artists' workshops were established in many parts of Africa, providing training in European media, techniques, and styles. Africans in increasing numbers have traveled abroad for their education, among them artists who absorb the lessons of European modernism and postmodernism just as Picasso and his peers once assimilated the lessons of African art into their own paintings. As the twenty-first century begins, African artists are dynamic members of a vibrant art scene that is increasingly global in its ideas, influences, and centers of activity.

Contexts, Styles, Artists

Most of the works of "classical" African art included in this catalogue were intended to be part of rituals, performances, and other contexts that relate directly to the lives of individuals and the livelihood of the communities for which they were made. Some African sculptures were made for rituals that promote human fertility, the continuity of the family, or the abundance of crops and other natural resources essential for survival. Others played important roles in the initiations that transformed young people into responsible adults. Still others assisted in honoring the dead and marking their transition to the world of the ancestors. Works of art in Africa proclaim the wisdom, wealth, and majesty of rulers and manifest the sacred power of the spirit world. Knowledge of the varied contexts in which these artworks were originally seen and used is essential to an appreciation of their forms and an understanding of their meanings.

In their original contexts, these artworks would appear much differently than they do photographed in this catalogue or on display in a museum – where they are isolated, static, silent, placed on a pedestal or in a showcase. Rather, the sculptures would be surrounded by many other objects in a shrine or a palace. They might be set in motion by the gestures of worshipers or courtiers. Their meanings would be expressed through spoken prayers, praises, or proverbs. Masks would assume just one small part of a multimedia spectacle featuring cloth, fiber, and many other costume elements, as well as music, dance, song, and the excitement of an enthralled crowd of spectators.

Seeing African art as it is shown here deprives us of the complex sensory atmosphere in which these objects were created and used, but allows us instead to focus on their formal elements and sculptural qualities. African sculptures are usually symmetrical, portraying figures in static, formal poses – either seated or standing – rather than engaged in dramatic action. They are not individualized portraits with specific and recognizable facial features, but rather generalized representations of people, usually in the prime of life.

African artists alter the appearance of the body in order to emphasize specific areas. The head is usually enlarged in proportion to the rest of the body, because of its primacy in terms of a person's moral and spiritual character. A female's breasts, belly, and buttocks may be exaggerated to emphasize her childbearing potential. Limbs, the torso, facial features, and other parts of the body are often reshaped to create dynamic, geometric forms.

Even though the objects in this catalogue are not identified by the names of the artists who created them, many people in their original communities would have known who they were. Unfortunately, Westerners have generally neglected to ascertain the names of the African artists who carved the objects they collect. Research over the past few decades has recovered some of the names. Probing the legacies of masters such as Bamgbose, the Yoruba artist believed to have carved the Epa helmet mask on p. 87, has revealed that individual innovation has been an important formative component of African art.

African artists are usually trained professionals, although they may not always practice their art as a full-time occupation. Among ethnic groups in the savanna region of West Africa (e.g., the Bamana and Senufo peoples), artists are members of hereditary groups who specialize in a particular medium and craft, such as ironwork, wood carving, brass casting, weaving, and pottery. Members of these hereditary artisan groups marry only among themselves and generally live somewhat apart from the non-artisan members of their ethnic group. Elsewhere, artists are drawn from specific families – as among the Yoruba – or are members of professional guilds, such as those who serve the royal court of Benin. In still other parts of Africa, the decision to become an artist is a personal one, independent of family lineage.

In all these cases, young people are trained by observing and assisting their elders from an early age, gradually learning the technique, forms, and ideas essential to their art. Throughout sub-Saharan Africa, the various arts have traditionally been open only to members of a particular gender. Wood carving, brass casting, ironwork, and some forms of weaving are done by men, while pottery, house painting, and other forms of weaving are the dominion of women.

In Africa today, there are both more and fewer opportunities for artists than existed a hundred years ago. Some of the clients who supported artists in the past – such as initiation associations, religious groups, or traditional political leaders – may no longer be as active as they once were. Their activities have been curtailed by the increase in Western-style education, conversions to Christianity and Islam, the presence of national and local governmental officials, and the many other changes in African culture. Yet despite these forces, the vast majority of the objects represented in this catalogue continue to have value and meaning for the peoples that created them.

There is incredible variety and vitality in African art today, as new markets, ideas, and modes of creating art are explored and adopted. Rather than declining, African art has become more complex in the past few decades. While artists retain many of the elements that have characterized their art forms in the past, they also seek new types of clients, use new materials and techniques (as well as adapting their old ones), and negotiate the difficult and often competing demands of tradition and modernity.

African art has always responded to change, reflecting the evolving religious, political, social, and intellectual values of its creators. In the act of changing, it preserves its essential nature as an active and vital part of the lives of its makers and users.

Kate Ezra
Coordinator of Art History,
Columbia College, Chicago

North Africa

The Tuareg live in a vast area stretching from the central Sahara desert southwards to the Niger River. Descendants of the Berbers, the indigenous population of North Africa, the Tuareg retain the Berber language but have adopted Islam and some aspects of Islamic culture. Their society is a hierarchy of nobility, priests, commoners, artisans, and slaves. The southern Tuareg were settled, while the Saharan Tuareg were nomadic herdsmen and, often, raiders of the desert camel caravans. They are well known for their indigo-dyed robes and for the veils that are worn (and rarely removed) by the men.

Islamic influence is evident in Tuareg art, which is based on simple design elements – mainly arcs, triangles, crosses, and circles. The Tuareg assembled these elements into complex compositions enhanced by a lavish use of brilliant primary colors: even their leather tents were stained red. Seemingly abstract, the designs all had roots in representations of natural forms. They were applied to practically every object in the limited range of Tuareg material culture, even sandals. Such combinations of designs are evident in this pair of posts, which were used as supports for cushions, to hang up bags, or to hold the interior mat walls of the tents in place.

Women worked leather into the cushions and heavily fringed bags, whereas men carved in wood the household equipment: beds (sometimes inlaid with metal), spoons, ladles, and mortars. Tuareg blacksmiths armed these warlike people with lances, daggers, and huge, medieval-type swords. Besides these military trappings, the Tuareg generally owned camel harnesses and a few domestic objects, such as pincers and hammers for breaking up lump sugar. Women's silver jewelry mainly consisted of triangular pendants with attached groups of smaller triangles. All of these were incised with the usual abstract designs.

The lock and keys shown on the following pages are an example of exceptional virtuosity in metalwork. A complex device in two metals, the lock requires a familiarity with its structure of multiple parts before it can be opened and closed – a procedure that sometimes involves as many as seven keys. These locks are used to secure the leather bags in which the Tuareg keep their valuables. Larger models of keys are hung on women's veils as emblems of high status. Like other elaborate metal objects possessed by the Tuareg, the locks and keys are probably the work of Sephardic Jewish metalworkers, many of whom practiced their skills in North African towns.

Gift of Denyse and Marc Ginzberg, New York, to American Friends of the Israel Museum

Gabus, 1958; *Prussin*, 1995; *Loughran*, 1995

Pair of support posts
Sahara region: Tuareg
Late 19th – early 20th century
Wood
Height 112, 108.5 cm
B98.0010 (a–b)

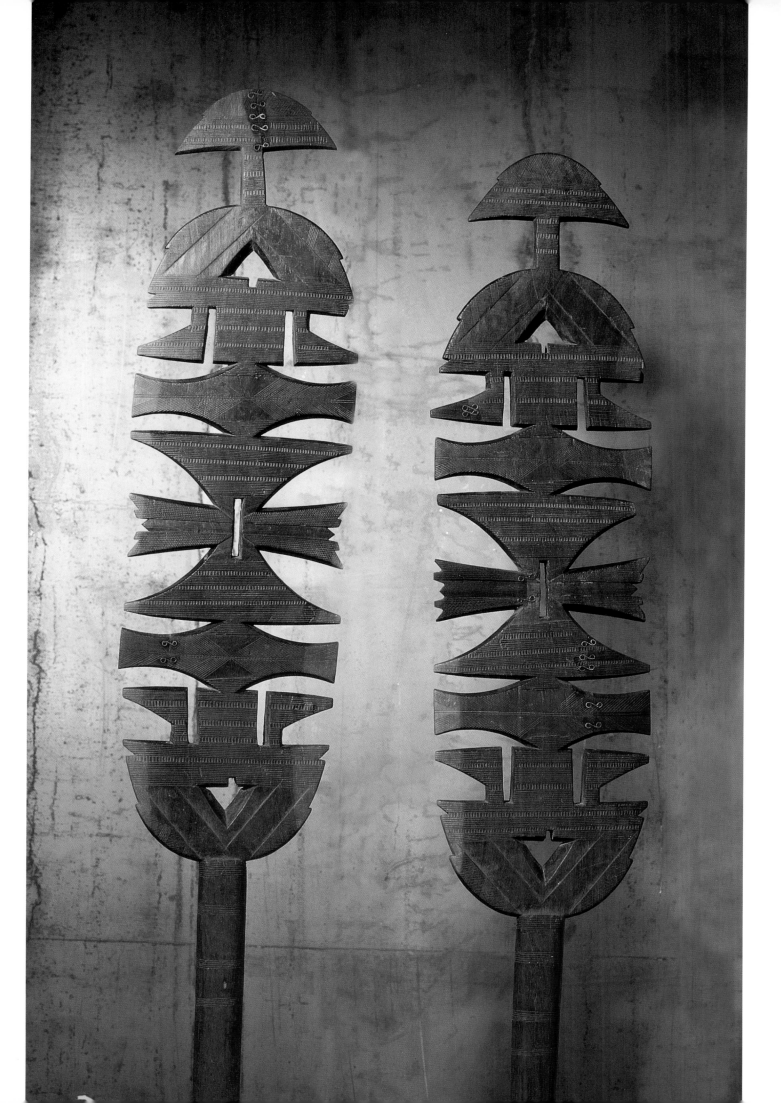

Lock and keys (*tanasi*)
Sahara region: Tuareg
Late 19th – early 20th century
Copper, brass, silver
Length: lock 14 cm; keys 13.5, 20.5 cm
B96.0603

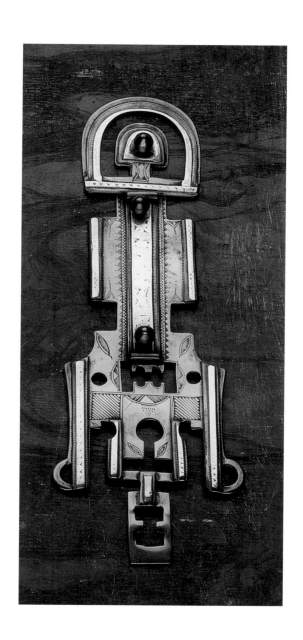

The Western Sudan

The little-known Sao culture had its inception in the area south of Lake Chad about 500 BCE. It reached its height some 400 to 1,000 years later, with large populations housed in walled cities. Among the Sao's artistic legacy were striking bronze ornaments and quantities of ceramic objects. The latter included half-length human figures, often wearing animal masks, and small heads of the present type, the meaning of which is completely unknown. For that matter, it is not even clear what they represent. Speculations as to whether their function was ritual or utilitarian – as weights for fishing nets, for example – are still unresolved.

Like Nigeria earlier, with its Nok culture, and Mali later, with the Jenne culture, western Niger had a rich early tradition of ceramic sculpture in the Bura region. Its center lay along the Niger River, at a point where it flows across the border of Mali and heads to the southeast. Among discoveries from several sites, the most remarkable so far have been made at Asinda-Sikka, a now-arid area that in ancient times was forested. Asinda-Sikka includes the remains of houses, ritual areas with altars built of large stone blocks, and a large cemetery with at least 630 burials. It is among these burials that ceramic sculptures have been found, though mostly in fragments.

Bones, especially skulls, were placed in large jars set upside down on the ground. The majority are tall cylinders topped with figures of horsemen; about a third are hemispherical, bearing either limbs and heads or heads only; and the least common are large and ovoid in form, surmounted with heads or whole figures.

The heads, set on long necks, may be rectangular and flat, or rounded, as in this case. Highly stylized, the noses are modeled as part of the basic form, but the other features are made with thin applied strips of clay. Scarification marks are also indicated by clay strips or incisions. Many heads and figures are decorated with modeled necklaces, brassards, and bracelets, the originals of which were probably made of metal: the Bura people are known to have used some iron tools and weapons, as well as copper ornaments. The figures of riders, in which the horses' heads display extraordinary elongation, show evidence of spectacularly elaborate harnesses.

Sao head: Promised gift of the Faith-dorian and Martin Wright Family, New York, to American Friends of the Israel Museum

Bura head: Gift of Pierre Amrouche, Paris

Jansen and Gauthier, 1973; *Lebeuf and Lebeuf*, 1977

Head
Chad: Sao culture
Ca. 500 CE
Clay
Height 7.6 cm

Head
Niger, Bura
Ca. 200–1000 CE
Clay
Height 20 cm
B96.0621

Muslim influence made itself felt in the Western Sudan as early as the eighth to the ninth century, and was formative in the creation of the area's early empires. Most likely spread through the presence of immigrating traders and craftsmen, the accession of Islam in the region did not inhibit the continuity of indigenous religions. Evidence for this comes in the form of numerous ceramic and bronze sculptures found at Jenne, a site named for an ancient city and culture in the Niger River valley. This culture appears to have flourished from about 700 to 1600.

Jenne ceramic sculpture demonstrates an astonishing array of subjects that include naturalistic single figures of horsemen, single male and female figures, and pairs of figures. Some are thought to be posed in ritually assumed attitudes (many still current today) that have been compared to Buddhist *mudra*s.

At the same time, the sculptures comprise a great variety of figures that presumably relate to deities, spirits, or other mythological beings. Many showing a grotesque, even monstrous, type of imagery were clearly cult objects, as they have been found on what appear to be altars. They include figures covered with what may be pronounced scarification marks or perhaps the pustules of disease. Some show snakes crawling on their bodies, and some female figures appear to be giving birth to snakes, creatures that in later times were associated with kingship. It has been suggested that some figures may have been made for a cult of a mother goddess, and this portrayal of a squatting elderly female is one of them. The funnel-like jaws are inexplicable, but suggest the head of a hippopotamus.

Gift of Philippe Guimiot and Marc L. Felix, Brussels

Seated female figure
Mali, Jenne-Jeno area
Ca. 1000–1300 CE
Clay
Height 41 cm
754.83

The arid land south of the Sahara in Mali, where the Dogon live, is dominated by a great stretch of cliffs known as the Bandiagara escarpment. Some of the Dogon villages are located on its plateau but the great majority are closely huddled at the foot of the heights. Others are built in the sandy Seno Plain that stretches eastward from Bandiagara.

Every Dogon village has an unwalled meeting house (*togu na*) for men, from which women are strictly excluded. These structures consist of rows of short pillars, of either wood or piled stones, that support a roof of millet-stalk thatch about two meters thick. The open construction and the dense roof provide a welcome coolness in this hot climate, and a place where men can sit (it is impossible to stand in them) for discussions of village affairs.

The Seno Plain is somewhat less dry than the cliff area, and supports more trees. Consequently the *togu na* built there tend to have broad wooden posts, forked at the top to support the roof beams. They are often carved with figures of men, women, or couples – probably associated with the mythical Nommo – displaying exaggerated sexual characteristics. The style is usually hard and angular, contrasting with the softer and more rounded forms of sculpture from the cliff area.

Gift of Mr. and Mrs. Fred Richman, New York, to American Friends of the Israel Museum

Huet, 1988

Post for *togu na* house
Mali: Dogon
Late 19th – early 20th century
Wood
Height 178 cm
189.84

When the horse was introduced to West Africa about 1,000 years ago, it became the prerogative of rulers and nobles. In sculpture its presence always denotes the depicted rider's high status. Among the Dogon, horses are principally the mounts of the powerful and revered *hogons*, male elders who are the religious and secular authorities of the community. The *hogons* also play a vital role as masters of the cult of Lebe, an ancestor whose function is the maintenance of fertility and regeneration – a crucial function to an agrarian culture in such an inhospitable environment.

In this sculpture, the rider wears the short fringe beard of elder men and carries as is done in life a sheathed knife on his left arm, which also holds the reins. Although several figures of this kind exist, they have not been fully investigated by researchers, and their significance is still undetermined. A number of suggestions include the claim that the personage is himself a *hogon*, or else an ancestor assuming the form of a *hogon*. He many even represent one of the ancestral Dogon who migrated to their present lands from the southwest some 500 years ago. In pose and attributes, the sculpture is highly reminiscent of ceramic horsemen made by the Jenne culture.

Gift of Mr. and Mrs. Philip Gersh, Los Angeles, to American Friends of the Israel Museum

Horseman
Mali: Dogon
19th century or earlier
Wood
Height 60 cm
916.78

The first Nommo, or ancestor of the Dogon, descended with his company of twin avatars from the heavens to the earth in an ark; upon their arrival, the Nommo transformed the ark into a horse that would draw them to their destination. This myth is commemorated in large, carved wooden troughs kept by the various Dogon lineage groups. Secret as well as sacred, they are used once a year in ceremonies honoring the creator Amma and the ancestors, during which they contain sacrificial meat that is distributed to the participants.

To an extent rare in African art, the trough is quite literally illustrative of the myth. The general form of the massive carving is a long, hollowed-out oblong, with a bridled horse's head at one end and its tail at the other. Both sides are carved in high relief with two groups of four Nommo twins, that is, the total assembly of original ancestors. The figures' arms are raised high in a gesture depicted over and over again in Dogon sculpture — probably signifying an appeal to Amma for the rain that provides water for humans, their animals, and, above all, their crops. A crocodile is placed between each pair; a beneficent creature who is a servant of the Nommo, the crocodile is often represented in masks as well. The chevron border around the edges illustrates the longed-for rain falling from the sky.

Gift of the Nelson Foundation, Greenwich, Connecticut, to American Friends of the Israel Museum, in memory of Nathan and Celia Birkman and Morris and Kate Nelson

Trough in the form of a horse
Mali: Dogon
Late 19th – early 20th century
Wood
Length 212 cm
B87.134

The Bozo live on the Niger River, near the Dogon and northeast of the Bamana; they are said to have been the earliest inhabitants of this area. The Bozo's way of life depends rather on fishing than agriculture, and their major cult is dedicated to Faro, a water spirit. Their sculpture finds its closest affinity in that of the Bamana, whose conventions it largely follows, but with the Bamana, tendency to formalism is often carried to an extreme. In some Bozo carvings, for instance, the human figure is reduced to planes set at right angles to one another and covered with geometric patterns.

This ram's head, however, is a fully realized piece of three-dimensional sculpture. It was originally a marionette, set on a handle that was manipulated by a dancer dressed in a concealing cloth costume. Together with other marionettes, it appeared on a portable platform in puppet shows at harvest and fishing festivals. The subject refers to the mythical ram that was sacrificed, for the first time this was done in the mythical past to neutralize the evil effects of a primeval woman's sins.

Gift of Jane Stern Lebell, New York, to American Friends of the Israel Museum

Marionette head of a ram (*saga*)
Mali, Mopti area: Bozo
Late 19th – early 20th century
Wood, paint, metal, cloth
Height 37 cm
B92.0821

Chi wara is the mythical "farming animal" who taught the Bamana the arts of agriculture that enabled them to survive in their harsh surroundings. The name is applied to a male association that seeks to emulate and personify the qualities of the *chi wara*, as well as to its ritual costumes and dances. The costumes are complete disguises made of long, flowing fibers; the wearers' heads are surmounted with crest carvings of antelopes. The dances are performed by pairs of farmers recognized for their superior skills, one with a male – and the other with a female – headpiece. Together they enact the movements of hoeing and the leaping of the animals.

The crests were carved in a number of different styles, according to the areas of their origins. The southern style is clearly less representational than those of the north and west. This crest, with its ridged and almost straight horns, depicts the head of a female oryx antelope; it would have had a male counterpart in the roan antelope.

This crest was carved in two pieces (as seen in other cases), the bell-shaped cap being one, and the antelope's neck, head, and horns, the other. Originally the two parts were secured with ties (which have now been eliminated) through carefully aligned holes, which are still apparent. This is an exceedingly rare and all but unique form.

Gift of Lawrence Gussman, Scarsdale, New York, to American Friends of the Israel Museum, in memory of Catharine R. Gussman

Dance crest (*chi wara*)
Mali: southern Bamana
Late 19th – early 20th century
Wood, cord, aluminum, snail shells
Height 66.8 cm
B98.0057

A suite of masquerades originated by the Wassalunke was adopted by their Bambana and Malinke neighbors. One set, called *koteba*, consisted of theatrical and satirical farces; the other, known as *wara*, employed animal masks, including the *sogoni koun* headpiece. Both sets were performed by young men of same–age group societies for the entertainment of people who employed them for temporary agricultural or other projects.

Nevertheless, for the Bamana the *sogoni koun* headpieces embodied rich symbolic meanings. Their design amalgamates abstracted images of three animals, identifiable even in the extremely simplified conformation of this example. The roan antelope appears as a lateral panel from which two pairs of horns arise (here considerably less curved than those of the actual animal). The semicircular form below shows a pangolin, a scaled, ant-eating mammal. This pangolin stands on a highly schematic representation of the aardvark – both of them are burrowing animals. This combination of animal elements manifests Bamana conceptions of cosmic and social action. The horns stand for the growth of millet – the Bamanas' staple crop – and the sun, which they perceive as male; the pangolin and aardvark symbolize the female earth. Their union, like the union of men and women, promotes fertility and the continuation of life. Originally the piece was attached to a small basketry cap that was placed on the wearer's head.

Gift of Faith-dorian and Martin Wright, New York, to American Friends of the Israel Museum, in memory of Abraham Janoff

Imperato, 1981

Dance crest (*sogoni koun*)
Mali: southern Wassalunke-Bamana
Late 19th – early 20th century
Wood
Height 29 cm
B93.1034

Little seems to be known about this type of mask. Its austerity closely parallels that of some Dogon masks, including the square apertures for eyes that also recall the architecture of windows in some of the great adobe buildings of Mali. Some masks of this kind are decorated with small metal plates or pieces of mirror, which are also a feature of Marka masks.

Gift of Faith-dorian and Martin Wright, New York, to American Friends of the Israel Museum, in memory of Abraham Janoff

Mask
Mali: Bamana or Marka
Late 19th – early 20th century
Wood
Height 49 cm
898.84

Senufo farmers have elevated their normal labors in the fields into a competitive test of men's physical prowess — and thus of their social worth. At a set time the young men of a village, or number of villages, assemble to try their strength. To the music of drums and xylophones, they toil against one another to determine which of them is the strongest and most successful at clearing and hoeing the land.

The winner at once becomes a man of great prestige in his society. As a champion, one of his rewards is to be presented with the *te fali pitya*, a carved staff topped with a small figure of an attractive young girl. The staff constitutes a broad hint to the winner and his village that he is now deserving of marriage to an actual girl who is equally desirable; their union will bring fertility and, thus, prosperity to the community. The staffs themselves are retained as heirlooms. They are placed at the door of a champion's house at his death, as a memorial of his achievement.

Gift of Faith-dorian and Martin Wright, New York, to American Friends of the Israel Museum, in memory of Abraham Janoff

Glaze, 1981

Champion cultivator's staff (*te fali pitya*)
Côte d'Ivoire: Senufo
Late 19th – early 20th century
Wood, iron, paint
Height 136 cm
899.84

The *kpeli-yehe* mask is an attribute of the Senufo form of Poro, a men's initiatory society of extensive influence in both secular and religious affairs. This widespread institution is found not only in the Côte d'Ivoire but, in various forms, in the neighboring countries of Liberia, Sierra Leone, and Guinea.

The Senufo mask appears at Poro initiations and at the funerals of its members. Its central feature is a human face bearing the welts of scarification. This is surrounded by symbolic elements. The leg-like forms below the face represent a stylization of a woman's coiffure – or may stand for the hornbill, the most important of the five animals first created by the gods. With its phallic beak and swollen pregnant belly, the hornbill is seen as an emblem of the union of male and female sexuality and birth. The horns above the brow are those of the ram, a sacrificial animal. The extension above the forehead may be still another phallic symbol.

Gift of Faith-dorian and Martin Wright, New York, to American Friends of the Israel Museum, in memory of Abraham Janoff

Bochet, 1993

Mask (*kpeli-yehe*)
Côte d'Ivoire: Senufo
Late 19th – early 20th century
Wood
Height 34 cm
893.84

Senufo helmet masks belong to small societies called Wabele or Wambele that are only loosely affiliated to the Poro, and whose paraphernalia were stored separately. The masks display a powerful combination of animal forms. From the central cap, a pair of long antelope horns sweeps out to the rear, framing (in sequence) a hornbill, a chameleon, and a pair of ram's horns in front of it – repeating the group of creatures shown on the *kpeli-yehe* mask (p. 00). Projecting to the front of the small eyes is a pair of broad jaws, sprouting curved tusks above and to the sides. These seem to allude to the hyena, hippopotamus, and crocodile. While the helmet mask was carried horizontally on the wearer's head, the rest of his body was concealed by a loose cotton costume.

The image is fearsome – and was intended to be. The mask was used as an instrument of terror, designed to dispel the forces of human sorcerers or of malevolent spirits. During its dance to the music of drums and singing, the mask was said to emit showers of sparks and swarms of bees from its jaws. In actuality, small cups of embers were placed in the jaws of the mask to produce this startling effect.

Gift of Charles Ratton, Paris

Glaze, 1981

Helmet mask (*kponyugu*)
Côte d'Ivoire: Senufo
Late 19th – early 20th century
Wood
Length 82 cm
950.78

In the Cercle de Bondoukou area, near the border of Ghana, a number of Muslim and non-Muslim groups live in close proximity, often sharing quarters in the same towns. In spite of their Muslim faith, the Dyula and Ligbi maintain a masked cult called Gbain, directed against the activities of witches, which also exists among such non-Muslims as the Kulango. The Dyula and Ligbi also perpetuate a masquerade called Do, in which a series of face masks is worn by members of their Do society for entertainment to mark such Muslim religious occasions as the end of Ramadan. The Do masks represent men and women, birds (thrushes and hornbills), and mammals (sheep, bush cows, and warthogs).

There has clearly been considerable cross-fertilization of styles, including influence from the Senufo, to whom some works from the area have formerly been credited. The style of the Kulango mask shown here is almost identical to that of the Dyula-Ligbi bush cow mask, which in turn has clear relationships to the Senufo *kpeli-yehe*. Again, the Gbain mask markedly resembles Senufo helmet masks.

The persistence of these essentially non-Muslim elements in Muslim society, the mutual respect among the groups, and the sense of their value that they continue to hold for all the communities are remarkable features of this region. Similar instances of cooperation and tolerance have also occurred among other Muslim groups in Côte d'Ivoire, Burkina Faso, Ghana, and Nigeria. These cases seem to be comparable to the climate of coexistence that evidently prevailed in Jenne many hundreds of years ago.

Anonymous gift to American Friends of the Israel Museum

Bravmann, 1974

Mask, bush cow
Côte d'Ivoire, Cercle de Bondoukou:
Kulango
Late 19th – early 20th century
Wood
Height 32.1 cm
B98.1058

The groups collectively referred to as Gurunsi migrated from northern Ghana. Today they live in an area that is largely forested, which in the past served as a haven from the onslaughts of the Mossi invaders. In spite of a lack of arable land, the Gurunsi are agriculturists who also depend on hunting and fishing. They maintain a classless society overseen by councils rather than chiefs or kings. The largest subgroup are the Nuna, with the smaller Nunuma, Winiama, Kisena, and Lela on their borders.

Yi is the Gurunsi's supreme being. Su — a part of Yi — is a spirit whose sphere of influence is the masks the Gurunsi use, and who is more or less spiritually present in all of them. There are two types of masks: one is connected to spirits of the bush, who are represented as a full menagerie of birds, animals, and reptiles; the second type is related to spirits who have no specific natural form.

Visually the most spectacular of the masks, the latter type is a variation on a theme that is also common to the Dogon and the northern Mossi (themselves probably of Dogon origin) and has been adopted by the Bobo and Bwa to the east of the Nuna. In all these areas, the mask has two parts: the face mask itself and an elongated vertical superstructure above it that assumes different forms locally. Among them are the slender, towering *sirigi* ("Mother of Masks") of the Dogon, and the *karanga* masks of the Mossi former kingdom of Yatenga, in northern Burkina Faso. Among the Gurunsi, Bobo, and Bwa, the masks have a flat, round face with a tall rectangular "plank" above it. The geometric patterns that embellish the planks are elements of a visual code revealing the mask's meaning to the initiated.

Some masks are sacred, made in response to supernatural orders; as protective beings, these are seen only at initiations, funerals, and an annual ritual for driving evil spirits from the village. Others, of exactly the same types, regularly appear in public as entertainers on market days and other such occasions.

Gift of Thomas G. B. Wheelock, New York, to American Friends of the Israel Museum, in honor of Martin Wright, and with the help of gifts from Fernandez Arman, New York; Dr. John and Nicole Dintenfass, New York; George Feher, New York; Hans Guggenheim, Boston; Dr. and Mrs. Alexander Honig, Riverdale, New York; Mr. and Mrs. Cedric H. Marks, New York; Ann Rogin and Rachel Adler, New York; the bequest of Bertha Abry; and the Arthur and Madeleine Chalette Lejwa Collection, bequeathed by Madeleine Chalette Lejwa to American Friends of the Israel Museum

Roy, 1987

Plank mask
Burkina Faso: Nuna
Late 19th — early 20th century
Wood, paint
Height 125 cm
B99.1336

The Mossi of today are descendants both of invaders from northern Ghana, who spread over the vast central plateau of Burkina Faso in the fifteenth to the sixteenth century, and of the original inhabitants. Formidable horsemen, the Nakomse conquerors subdued or expelled the native Nyonyose and established several kingdoms, the most powerful based in Ouagadougou, the present capital.

Varying artistic styles are found in the areas of each kingdom, pointing to the differences between the art of the Nakomse and Nyonyose; specifically, the former stress figural sculpture, and the latter, masks (*wango*). Among the Ouagadougou people, masks include both face masks and horizontal headpieces, usually quite small in scale. The masks are worn with costumes consisting of enormous bundles of fiber that seem to swell the wearer's body hugely, concealing all but his hands and feet. Each mask, whether human or animal (in this case the creature represented is the duyker, a small antelope), refers to a being that figures in the myth of origin of a particular clan.

Gift of Thomas G. B. Wheelock, New York, to American Friends of the Israel Museum, in honor of Martin Wright, and with the help of gifts from Mr. and Mrs. David Heller, Woodmere, New York; Dr. and Mrs. Itzicowitz, Paris; Dr. and Mrs. Milton Ratner, New York; Mr. and Mrs. Gustave Schindler, New York; Mr. and Mrs. Marc Sherman, New York; Mr. and Mrs. Daniel Slott, New York; and Mr. and Mrs. Roger Stoll, New York, to American Friends of the Israel Museum

Roy, 1987

Antelope headpiece (*wan[go]-nyaka*)
Burkina Faso, Ouagadougou area: Mossi
Late 19th – early 20th century
Wood, paint
Height 62 cm
B00.1547

The Lobi migrated westward from Ghana towards the end of the eighteenth century, later spreading north and south; they are now interspersed among other groups, namely the Gan, Dioula, and Birifor. Their communities consist of widely spaced, large houses built of adobe with terraced roofs, each containing a number of rooms that accommodate the extended family. In the absence of chiefdoms or similar foci of authority, the family head regulates affairs.

Each house includes a shrine room containing a host of wood or ceramic figures. There are also open-air shrines peopled with large clay figures and wooden heads in the ground or on the house walls, serving as guardian spirits. The figures of the house shrines are made for, and at the behest of, the spirits called *thila*. *Thila* are the intermediaries between the Creator and man; it is left to diviners to interpret their wishes and actions.

The majority of Lobi sculptures are standing male and female figures carved in a markedly austere and static style that minimizes anatomical detail – except for facial features – and envelops the body in smooth surfaces. The frequently heavy upper eyelids reinforce this impression of stasis and remoteness. Some, however, have one or both arms raised in gestures of appeal for the relief of anguish; others are double-headed or paired figures, sometimes in copulation.

Gift of Mr. and Mrs. Gustave Schindler, New York, to American Friends of the Israel Museum

Meyer, 1981

Pair of figures (*bateba*)
Côte d'Ivoire–Burkina Faso: Lobi
Late 19th – early 20th century
Wood
Height: female 75.6 cm; male 73 cm
B85.0080(a–b)

The Moba live in the north of two adjoining countries, Togo and Ghana; they are primarily agriculturists but also rely on hunting. Their art is confined to metalworking, for small ornaments, and the sculpture in wood of large and small human figures called *tchitcherik* (pl., *tchitcheri*). These figures are perhaps the most rigorously stylized works of the entire range of African art. In their reductive portrayal of the human form, facial features, fingers, and toes are all omitted – even gender is rarely indicated. They would seem to have more in common with the styles of Burkina Faso and Mali than with any others.

Though always conforming to a single formula, *tchitcheri* fall into several named types, distinguished largely on the basis of size and function. The larger figures, *tchitcheri sakab* ("old men" *tchitcheri*), represent the immediate ancestors of the head of a family group. These figures are placed upright on the ground, often partly buried. Others are hung on walls or trees near the shrines where sacrifices are made to the ancestors.

Gift of Pierre Amrouche, Paris

Kreamer, 1987

Figure (*tchitcherik*)
Togo-Ghana: Moba
Late 19th – early 20th century
Wood
Height 91 cm
B93.1033

The Guinea Coast

The Bidyogo live on the Bissagos Islands opposite the coast of Guinea-Bissau. They are best known for their naturalistic masks, worn preceding initiations, representing animals (particularly oxen), sharks, and sawfish. Human figures, showing a creator god, are frequently formalistic to the point of abstraction.

Spoons used on ceremonial occasions for the serving of rice — the staple food of the Bidyogo people — have shafts carved as female figures, sometimes merely indicated by breasts and a skirt or by a half-length figure. This spoon is unusual in its realistic portrayal of a young woman. The handle ends in a spatula, used for loosening rice stuck to the sides of the cooking vessel.

Similar figures are also to be found on staffs used in boys' initiation ceremonies and on ceremonial axes carried by women during rituals in which they are possessed by male spirits.

Gift of Mr. and Mrs. Samuel Dubiner, Ramat Gan

Spoon
Guinea-Bissau: Bidyogo
Late 19th — early 20th century
Wood
Height 52 cm
1043.2.56

The Mende invaded Sierra Leone in the mid-sixteenth century, and have exercised great influence on the indigenous groups, such as the Temne. Among both Mende and Temne, women have a major secret society (one of several), called Bundu or Sande, that is equivalent to the men's society, Poro. The society is unique in West Africa in that its female members commission, and wear, helmet masks from male carvers.

The figure shown here was probably made for the Yassi society of women diviners. Like some others of its kind, the figure is rendered in a more delicate and graceful style than the usually coarse Mende forms, and more closely approaches the figure sculpture of the Baga to the west.

The small face and coiffure seen here also exist in the Sowo masks of the Sande. The ringed neck is a feature appearing in the masks and other sculptures of the Mende, for whom it expresses prosperity and fertility. In a living woman, encircling lines on a long neck are the epitome of feminine beauty. Additionally, they are one of the attributes of Tingoi, a water spirit who embodies physical beauty and appears in dreams to those she favors.

Gift of Mr. and Mrs. Joseph Gerofsky, New York, to American Friends of the Israel Museum

Boone, 1986

Female figure
Sierra Leone: Mende
Late 19th – early 20th century
Wood
Height 81 cm
174.84

The Dan are a large group of agricultural people living in mountain and savanna areas; villagers without a central authority, they were formerly known for their warring against surrounding groups.

The Dan carve countless examples of masks in a great number of types, which function in many contexts – from social control to entertainment. Some small female figures are cast in metal; figure sculpture in wood is rare, and considered to be an accomplishment of only the most skillful and esteemed master artists.

Such figures always represent nude women, standing in a stiffly upright pose, limbs spread away from the body. They are stained a glossy black, sometimes with colored details of facial paint. The faces are mask-like (in fact, they replicate the features of one type of mask) with slit eyes, full lips, and inset metal teeth. Plaited caps mimic actual women's coiffures, and the scarification patterns on the figures' torsos reflect those on the bodies of real women. All in all, the figures exemplify the Dan's ideal standard of feminine beauty.

As works of master carvers, these figures were costly, and consequently only made on commissions from wealthy men. Although they were never conceived to be literal portraits, they were meant to commemorate and celebrate the charms of favorite wives. As such, they were treasured possessions, normally kept carefully hidden away – but on occasion displayed with pride (and with the wives' permission) to privileged guests.

Gift of Faith-dorian and Martin Wright, New York, to American Friends of the Israel Museum, in memory of Abraham Janoff

Fischer and Himmelheber, 1976

Female figure (*lu me*)
Liberia or Côte d'Ivoire: Dan
Late 19th – early 20th century
Wood
Height 40 cm
B92.1591

The Guro, in company with the Dan, with whom they still maintain close contact, migrated to the Côte d'Ivoire from the north. The Guro now live around the Red Bandama River, with the Baule to their east. The art of the Guro – the masks in particular – now has a much more obvious affinity to the Baule's than to that of the Dan.

Guro clans are proprietors of *yu*, a term applied to religious and political associations and their paraphernalia. One of the most important *yu* of the northern Guro includes a group of masks that show certain similarities to the Baule performance of Goli. Here, again, is a group of beings that stand in a familial relationship to one another, though they are fewer in number than the Baule's and their personalities are less rigorously defined. The father is *zahuli*, a mask somewhat resembling *goli*; his wife is *zamble*, who wears an elegant mask of an antelope; and their daughter wears the *gu* mask of a beautiful woman. But these roles are mutable: should *zahuli* not appear at a performance, *zamble* may then be the husband and *gu*, the wife.

Gu masks wear coiffures indicating the status of the families that own them; the parted lips also disclose the filed teeth that were formerly a mark of feminine elegance and attractiveness. A group of *gu* masks featuring the concentric semicircles around the eyes and on the cheeks that appear on this one, is attributed to the "Master of Goitafla" (*fla* = village), in the northeastern Guro area.

The Arthur and Madeleine Chalette Lejwa Collection, bequeathed by Madeleine Chalette Lejwa to American Friends of the Israel Museum

Deluz, 1993; *Fischer and Homberger*, 1985

Mask (*gu*)
Côte d'Ivoire: Guro
Wood, paint
Late 19th – early 20th century
Height 46 cm
B00.0660

The Baule have an exceptionally rich tradition of wood carving, both for religious and purely decorative purposes. Its repertoire has been changed and enriched by the retention of old forms and the acquisition of new. The Baule's figure sculpture is now among the most famous from Africa for its naturalism, grace, and meticulous attention to detail. It consists largely of statuettes of men and women, sitting or standing, which have a specialized function.

While the Baule maintain a conception of creative divinities, these are never represented in tangible form. Figure sculpture, however, plays an intimate role in Baule thought and life. In the first place, it is believed that the present world is inhabited by spirits of earth, water, forests, and fields, as well as others who are mischievous or even malevolent. There is also a spirit world, duplicating that of humanity, from which people come at birth and to which they return at death. In the act of birth, people necessarily abandon their families in the spirit world.

Figures, then, are carved to represent nature spirits (*asye usu*) – who sometimes become the companions of human beings – or to house the spirits of spouses who have been left behind in the other world. The males are called *blolo bian*, and the females, *blolo bla*. In style, the nature spirit and spouse figures are visually indistinguishable. Spirit spouse figures are kept in their owners' sleeping rooms, though women in particular may sometimes carry their "spirit husbands" about with them.

The figures are generally shown as nude but are decorated with bead ornaments. Naturally enough, they accord with Baule standards of physical beauty, as in the case of this young woman, who has the small breasts and slender torso of youth and the sturdy legs needed for agricultural work.

Gift of Gaston de Havenon, New York, to American Friends of the Israel Museum

Ravenhill, 1980; *Vogel*, 1980

Female figure
Côte d'Ivoire: Baule
Late 19th – early 20th century
Wood, beads, string
Height 44 cm
592.81

In many parts of Africa the exterior surfaces of doors and shutters were frequently carved with abstract relief designs; figurative images, such as were used by the Dogon, Senufo, and Baule, were much rarer. Among the Baule, at least, the art of decorating doors is now extinct.

Animals were a favorite theme, particularly fish, animals, and crocodiles; these were shown in the same iconographic forms as can be seen in the small metal weights used for measuring gold dust. This example shows three subjects: a bird, seen in silhouette, as if from above or below; an antelope in profile; and a human face in the style of a mask. While quite detached from one another, the three images create a unified composition through the interplay of the two vertical images with the interposed horizontal of the antelope.

Gift of Mr. and Mrs. Herbert Baker, Los Angeles, to American Friends of the Israel Museum

Door
Côte d'Ivoire: Baule
Late 19th – early 20th century
Wood, paint
Height 153 cm
187.84

Besides doors, Baule houses were also decorated with small, carved shutters. This example is one of a pair that appears to have been made by the same sculptor. The central feature of each is the representation of a mask, protruding from the panel on a short, cylindrical shaft.

The mask in this case is related to a type representing the moon that appears at the beginning of a dance entertainment called Gbagba. The mask on the companion shutter, however, is modeled on the most sacred mask – a male secret, the sight of which is forbidden to women. Its appearance in this context, and on other such highly visible objects as weights, gong-beaters, and heddle-pulleys, is based on the assumption that women will not recognize its true nature.

Formerly in the Helena Rubinstein Collection
The Arthur and Madeleine Chalette Lejwa Collection, bequeathed by Madeleine Chalette Lejwa to American Friends of the Israel Museum

Vogel, 1997

Shutter
Côte d'Ivoire: Baule
Late 19th – early 20th century
Wood, paint
Height 54.5 cm
B00.0678

Among other types of masks, the Baule have an entire group collectively known as Goli, which is considered as a family. The performance in which they appear, also known as Goli, was introduced about the last decade of the nineteenth century by a neighboring group, the Wan. The Baule have made their own adjustments to the program and also, presumably, to its original meaning. While the performance today sometimes takes place at the funerals of important men, generally speaking it is carried out purely (and frequently) as a very popular form of entertainment.

The personae of Goli are two males and two females, each embodied in a pair of masks of the same form; in successive order, the males appear first, the females after. The masks evince a certain ambiguity: they all possess male and female aspects, or perhaps two complementary aspects of a single being.

The first to appear are the junior males, *kple kple* (the abstract mask shown here), representing perhaps the son of the family. *Kple kple* can be colored red, indicating a female, or black, denoting a male. Next is the father or senior male, *goli glen*, a zoomorphic image resembling the head of a bush cow with the horns of a gazelle. The junior female masks, following next, are *kpan pre*. In striking contrast to the abstraction of the male masks, these face masks are naturalistic, with small, backward-pointing horns. The last pair of masks, the senior females, are the *kpan*, which feature a beautiful human face crowned with one or the other of the elaborate coiffures worn by Baule women. All the maskers wear a fiber costume that conceals the dancer's entire body, with an animal skin hung on the back.

The sequence in which the masks appear is significant, since it implies a hierarchy in which females are tacitly acknowledged as truly the most powerful beings in the world.

Kple kple's flatness and geometric austerity form a striking contrast to the full volumes and studied beauty of Baule figural sculpture and the naturalistic charm of the *kpan* mask. *Goli glen*, though three-dimensional, is also harshly angular. Both these types of masks seem foreign to the gracious

Mask (*kple kple* or *kwasi gbe*)
Côte d'Ivoire: Baule
Late 19th – early 20th century
Wood, paint
Height 38 cm
B97.0003

expression of human physical beauty that is so notable in the Baule aesthetic universe. They are reminiscent, rather, of the much starker styles of the lands to the north and east: specifically, *kple kple* recalls the disk faces of the Nuna masks (p. 51), while *goli glen* seems to belong to the tradition of horizontal headpieces or masks, such as those of the Senufo (p. 47).

Kple kple mask: Gift of Lawrence Gussman, Scarsdale, New York, to American Friends of the Israel Museum, in memory of Catharine R. Gussman

Goli glen mask: Formerly in the Paul Guillaume and Nelson A. Rockefeller Collections
The Arthur and Madeleine Chalette Lejwa Collection, bequeathed by Madeleine Chalette Lejwa to American Friends of the Israel Museum

Kple kple: Boyer, 1993; *Vogel*, 1997; *Goli glen: McNaughton*, 1991; *Vogel*, 1997

Mask (*goli glen*)
Côte d'Ivoire: Baule
Late 19th - early 20th century
Wood, paint
Height 87.5 cm
B00.0659

Made for either men or women, Akan ceramic heads were memorial images intended as specific representations of the deceased, showing, for instance, his or her individual hairstyle, scarification marks, and even skin tone. In some Akan groups, everyone except a child had the right to such an image; in others, they were the privilege of only royal persons. These sculptures are exceptional in African art for being made exclusively by women ceramists; wood sculpture, on the other hand, was the work of Akan men. The artist was in attendance at the dying person's deathbed, and later fortified her memory of his or her appearance through divinatory ceremonies. Her work was conducted in strict secrecy.

The head was made to provide a home for the deceased's spirit, which was invoked to occupy it in a ceremony held by the congregated women of the village. It was then installed at a site near the village along with all the preceding *mma*, and offerings were made to them there. Besides their memorial functions, *mma* were believed to promote fertility.

The dating of these objects is uncertain, though some have been found in archaeological contexts. The tradition may have begun in the area about the late seventeenth century, but has now been defunct for over fifty years. While it lasted, the heads were made in a number of different local styles.

Gift of Mr. and Mrs. Gustave Schindler, New York, to American Friends of the Israel Museum

Sieber, 1973

Memorial head (*mma*)
Ghana: Akan
Late 19th – early 20th century
Clay, paint
Height 25 cm
563.84

In Ghana, part of what was once called the Gold Coast, the art of the Asante court was notable for its splendor; royal paraphernalia, which included rich textiles, employed an ostentatious display of gold and silver.

The small figures known as *akua'maa* (sing., *akua'ba*) represent a more intimate aspect of Asante familial life and art. The *akua'ba* was an object, sanctified by a priest, that embodied a young woman's hope of fertility and her future child itself; she carried the figure on her back and treated it much as she would a real child.

These figures were of the utmost formal simplicity, being no more that the conjunction of a circle and a cross (a satisfying geometrical combination, as many other cultures have found). Yet with all its lack of naturalism, the *akua'ba* expresses in visual terms the mother's wishes for her future child's beauty and well-being: the flatness of the high, round head stands for the flatness she will induce by massaging the soft skull; the corrugated neck bespeaks the fat folds of a well-fed child; and the beads signify material prosperity. Above all, the figure's small breasts symbolize the function of women, who are viewed in this matriarchal society as the channels through which humanity perpetuates itself from generation to generation.

Gift of Dr. Israel and Michaella Samuelly, Brooklyn, New York, to American Friends of the Israel Museum

Sieber, 1973

Doll (*akua'ba*)
Ghana: Akan, Asante people
Late 19th – early 20th century
Wood, paint
Height 32.5 cm
B00.1702

Nigeria

The Nok culture (so called after the first site where its relics were discovered) extended across a large swath of northern Nigeria, beginning in the first millennium BCE. At that time the area was probably more forested than it is today and must have harbored abundant wildlife. The people used stone tools, including arrowheads for hunting and hoes for cultivation. It appears that by about 400–200 BCE, they were smelting and working iron in considerable quantities. They had also become highly skilled at working in clay, not only for domestic pottery but for sculpture. Their works included animal figures of elephants, monkeys, and snakes, and above all, human images.

The Nok figures are the earliest sculptures known from sub-Saharan Africa. Though most are quite small, some fragments are evidence that the Nok people were capable of making whole figures well over a meter high. The heads show all but uniform features. They are generally spherical or cylindrical, with triangular eyes under arched eyebrows, straight noses with flared nostrils, and large, everted lips. The mouths, ears, nostrils, and eyes are perforated.

While the Nok people may not have worn fabrics (they probably clothed themselves in animal hides and bark-cloth), they engaged in a high degree of personal ornamentation. Coiffures were elaborate, with hair puffed or trimmed into shape. Men wore nose-plugs, and beads were used in profuse quantities as necklaces, sporrans, bracelets, and anklets. This imposing figure demonstrates the elaboration of Nok attire. Probably once housed in a shrine, it has its right arm raised in what appears to be a gesture of command.

Gift of Alain de Monbrison, Paris

Eyo and Willett, 1980; *de Grunne*, 1988

Figure
Nigeria: Nok culture
Ca. 500 BCE – 200 CE
Clay
Height 67 cm
B00.0634

The actual origin of the kingdom of Ife, or Ile-Ife, in central Nigeria is obscure; the Yoruba people who founded it may have been immigrants to the area about 350 BCE. Among all the Yoruba, however, the city of Ife has great mythological and religious prestige. The legend goes that Olodumare, the creator, sent his son Oduduwa to make the world, and that in due course Oduduwa became the first Oni, or king, of Ife. Other sons of Olodumare set up other kingdoms, and thus their rulers, including those of Benin, consider the Oni of Ife their elder brother.

Tradition tells us that during the reign of the third Oni, Obalufon, the Ife learned the art of casting in metal, perhaps from craftsmen journeying from the southern Sahara. About thirty such castings are known today. The majority form a group of copper or brass heads unparalleled elsewhere in Africa. The castings are portraits, rendered with great individuality and nobility, unquestionably of recognizable persons. They seem to have been used as supports for regalia during annual royal ceremonies of renewal held for Onis.

It is likely that, prior to learning metalwork, the people of Ife were already using ceramics for sculpture in a naturalistic style, which they later adapted to brass-casting. The numerous surviving ceramic sculptures were kept in sacred groves around the city or were buried in royal graves. They portray many subjects, both animal and human, but the great majority of them are heads. Some of them clearly predate the metal sculptures, while others are contemporary with them, and may well have been made by the same artists.

Many of the ceramics are fragments. In this example the head is an independent piece, not a fragment of a larger figure, and retains traces of its original coating of red paint.

Gift of Pierre Amrouche, Paris, and Lance Entwistle and Co., London, in honor of Martin Wright, and with the help of gifts from Renee and Chaim Gross; Curtis Katz and family; the Nash Family Foundation, Inc.; the Faith-dorian and Martin Wright Family; and an anonymous donor, to American Friends of the Israel Museum

Drewal, Pemberton, and Abiodun, 1989; *Eyo and Willett*, 1980; *Willett*, 1961

Head
Nigeria, Ile-Ife kingdom: Yoruba
Ca. 12th–15th century
Clay, paint
Height 15.3 cm
B95.0145

Benin, a kingdom to the southeast of Yoruba country with its capital at the city of that name, began its ascent to power about 1300 CE. Under the leadership of a succession of energetic rulers, the Obas, Benin rapidly gained an authority that extended far beyond its original borders. The arrival from Europe of the first Portuguese – and, later, Spanish – traders at the end of the fifteenth century increased the kingdom's growing commercial strength and wealth.

The Oba, reputed to be descended from the son of a god, and considered divine in his own right, had absolute control over his subjects. This extended to direct ownership of many products of their specialized skills. The art of brass-casting, said to have been acquired from the ancient city of Ife about 1400, was one of the Oba's monopolies, as was work in ivory. The workers were concentrated in compounds in his palace, and it is precisely in these two materials that Benin artists achieved their greatest triumphs in what is essentially a school of hieratic court art. The pictorial brass reliefs for the palace's columns and the heads of Obas for their ancestral altars are among the most renowned African masterpieces. At the same time, a wealth of minor objects were cast in brass, including bells, staffs, vessels, and small pendant masks and plaques.

This plaque shows three figures, presented frontally. The subject – showing an Oba flanked by two attendants, who support his arms with their hands on his hands and elbows – recurs frequently in Benin art. The three figures are dressed identically, with short kilts and headdresses and chokers of precious coral beads. Indeed, the group of three has a double significance. On the one hand, three is a number that symbolizes the king's destructive ability to inflict harm. At the same time, the trio in this image signifies the Oba's dependence upon the support of his allies.

The lower part of the plaque, which was originally semicircular in shape, has been lost.

Gift of Dr. and Mrs. Daniel Solomon, Los Angeles, to American Friends of the Israel Museum

Ezra, 1992

Plaque pendant
Nigeria, Court of Benin: Edo
Ca. 17th century
Brass
Height 15 cm
778.83

The Yoruba of western Nigeria number about ten million people, divided among small kingdoms or city-states under sacred rulers who govern through a body of nobles, aided by councils of elders. Always immensely prolific artists in all media, the Yoruba's greatest achievements have been in wood – with works that include architectural pieces, figures, and masks. According to Yoruba belief, the supernatural world, which is populated by deified ancestors and spirits, is constantly interacting with the human world through reincarnation, ritual, and divination. Sculptures, used as altar equipment and appearing in public pageants and festivals, are one of the channels for this communication.

There are many local carving styles in Yoruba country, as well as many types of performances. Among them are the enormous masks, carved from single blocks of wood, that are made for the Epa festival of the Ekiti kingdoms of the northeastern region. The base of these masks is a helmet that fits over the wearer's head, carved as a broadly designed human face representing the dead. This supports a thin platform on which stands the superstructure of figures, carved in the round, that forms the true subject of the mask. Several such masks are used at the festival, where they appear in a more or less set order.

The first is called Oloko. This mask shows a leopard savaging an antelope, and its masquerader dances vigorously to imitate the feline's leaps. Oloko refers to the peoples' hunting and agricultural skills. It is followed by masks showing figures of warriors on horseback carrying spears, the traditional weapons of the military guardians of the state. Next there appear masks with figures of priests, the peoples' spiritual guardians. Next to last come the Eyalase ("woman possessing power") masks, depicting women carrying royal emblems, accompanied by their children. With them, or finally, comes Orangun, a magnificent composition of a richly caparisoned warrior king mounted on his horse, surrounded by a whole crowd of atttendants. As a complete group, the masks express human history, from the simple energies of nature, through civilizing influences, to the interdependent forces relating males and females.

This mask is the work of the famous sculptor Bamgbose, perhaps carved about 1930.

Gift of Gaston de Havenon, New York, to American Friends of the Israel Museum

Thompson, 1974; Bamgbose: *John Picton* (personal communication)

"Eyalase" helmet mask for the
Epa festival
Nigeria, Osi-Ilorin: Yoruba
Carved ca. 1930
Wood, paint
Height 103 cm
920.78

High-status families in Yoruba country, like the rulers themselves, have altars in their houses dedicated to their ancestors. In Owo, as in other Yoruba kingdoms, and among the neighboring Ishan, the altars carry carved wooden heads on disk-shaped bases, showing the horned heads of rams or human heads bearing rams' horns. The horns symbolize the aggressive strength of the animal, also conceived as an attribute of the human forebear. Behind each head there is usually a hollow tube or slot in which a stick may be rattled to invoke the ancestor's presence and attention.

Gift of Howard Nelson, Greenwich, New Jersey, to American Friends of the Israel Museum

Ram's head (*osanmasinmi*)
Nigeria, Owo kingdom: Yoruba
Late 19th – early 20th century
Wood
Height 41 cm
B92.1527

In legendary times, Shango was the fourth ruler of the kingdom of Oyo-Ile. Angered by his subjects, he went into self-exile and died far away by his own hand. The thunderstorms that he had caused by magic in his lifetime continued even after his death; finally his former subjects concluded that Shango was indeed a god, and established his cult. The symbol of Shango is a pair of Neolithic stone blades, such as are sometimes turned up in fields during agricultural work; they are believed to be his thunderbolts.

In this figure we see a woman devotee of Shango, nude except for a bead-belt, carrying a double ax shape — symbolizing his thunderbolts — on her head. She is half-kneeling, but supported by a stylized "mudfish," a royal emblem. In front of her she holds an offering bowl that rests on her thighs. On her back she carries a child wearing a hood, head turned to the left, and reaching under her left arm to cling to her shoulder. Such figures are placed in the shrines of Shango to gain his protection. Ritual staffs with short handles, carried at dances in honor of Shango, sometimes bear the same figural group.

Shango is an equivocal and unpredictable god who continues to exercise the dangerous powers he wielded during his lifetime on earth. There are two aspects of his activities. The storms of thunder and lightning he inflicts on humanity are destructive and ruinous; on the other hand, the rain that he also controls is fructifying and necessary for fertility. Thus, it is appropriate for female devotees and priestesses, whose role as women is also to promote fertility, to serve Shango and to become possessed by his spirit during ritual.

Figure for a shrine to Shango
Nigeria, probably Oshogbo: Yoruba
Late 19th – early 20th century
Wood
Height 15.5 cm
L-B86.60

Beads of various kinds have been used by the Yoruba for centuries as enhancement for royal and ritual objects. Their use has been seen in objects as diverse as crowns, caps, bags for divining equipment, parts of costumes (including shoes and sashes), footstools, sheaths for the huge metal staffs symbolizing the god Oko, ceremonial swords, and garments for the small wooden figures (*ibeji*) of deceased twins. The crowns, in particular, often incorporated small, entirely three-dimensional beaded figures of animals and humans.

The art of beadwork seems to have gained impetus among the Yoruba when tiny beads were introduced in trade from Europe during the second half of the nineteenth century; thereafter, it flourished in ever more elaborated forms. It seems that the actual colors of the beads, as well as the patterns in which they are worked, carry powerful allusions to specific gods and their myths.

Gift of Lisa Bradley, New York, to American Friends of the Israel Museum, in honor of Ruth Popkin

Fagg, 1980

Crown
Nigeria: Yoruba
19th–20th century
Beads, cloth
Height 20 cm
B97.0022

This extraordinary vessel, probably used as an oil lamp, is composed of a female figure with prominent breasts, her arms supporting a shallow, footed bowl which takes the place of her head. This is raised on several notched struts which in turn incorporate smaller bowls. The struts stand on the perimeter of yet another, larger, footed bowl which repeats the form of the "head."

Few others of this type seem to exist apart from one in a French private collecion and another formerly in the Barbier-Mueller collection (now in the Musée National des Arts d'Afrique et d'Océanie, Paris). The latter has been attributed to the Yoruba. However, given the sculptural skills of Akan women ceramists (illustrated by the head shown on p. 77), and a number of formal points (including the shape and decoration of the lowest bowl), an Akan origin for this work seems likely.

Gift of Mr. and Mrs. Gustave Schindler, New York, to American Friends of the Israel Museum

Vessel
Probably Ghana: Akan
Clay
Height 30 cm
561.84

Masks and masquerades, almost ubiquitous throughout sub-Saharan Africa, are nowhere more so than among the Igbo. It is estimated that the Igbo have hundreds of types of masks. Most of them are not completely standardized, owing to variations in the different areas of Igbo country, as well as to the fertility of individual artists' creative imaginations. There has also been considerable cross-fertilization of mask types between the Igbo and neighboring peoples. The Igbo's masks are all, to a greater or lesser extent, personifications of spirits. They are present for every significant episode of life, from initiation to death. They appear in large numbers, to the accompaniment of orchestras and choirs, greeted by the enthusiasm of crowds of spectators.

While the subjects of the masks encompass the entire spectrum of Igbo life, they appear to express a pervasive thematic dualism – of youth and age, male and female, beauty and force. Female youth and beauty are embodied in "maiden" masks worn with elegant costumes. Male force is expressed by the mask type known as *mgbedike*, worn by mature men celebrated as farmers, hunters, and, formerly, warriors. These masks are characterized by huge mouths with prominent bared teeth and two large pairs of horns, often with subsidiary figures between them. There are many variations on this theme, some extremely elaborate, incorporating additional carvings and a wide range of natural materials. The costume, covering the entire body, bristles with porcupine quills and clatters with rattles. While not malevolent, the *mgbedike* masks – in keeping with the actions and dances of their wearers – display energy and aggression carried to the point of violence.

Gift of Mr. and Mrs. Joseph Gerofsky, New York, to American Friends of the Israel Museum

Cole and Aniakor, 1984

Mask (*mgbedike*)
Nigeria: Igbo, north central area
Late 19th – early 20th century
Wood, paint
Height 60 cm
173.84

The Ibibio, living in the delta of the Niger River, have several men's societies, some indigenous, others adopted from neighboring groups. They have different functions. For instance, the important Ekpo society is an ancestral cult celebrated annually, when its masked members appear in public. The masks may be elegant or grotesque; the latter are feared, since they are purported to exercise control over, and punish, wrongdoers of both sexes.

The Ekon society is composed of young men, and its power is demonstrated in a very unconventional – albeit effective – manner. Formed into troupes, the members travel every seven years from village to village presenting entertainment in the form of dances, songs, and marionette playlets. The marionette performances are enacted on platforms, and require considerable skill in the manipulation of the articulated wood figures. The dialogue of the skits is delivered by men with disguised voices, and the content is highly satirical commentary – to the point of obscenity – on current events and well-known personalities. If the Ekpo society penalizes its delinquent members through terror, the Ekon society exposes them to public ridicule and shame.

The techniques of articulation and compositions of separate parts used in the marionettes are employed in other Ibibio figure sculptures, including memorial images of notable men. These techniques were probably introduced through imitation of European carpentry methods.

Gift of Jerome Joss, Sherman Oaks, California, to American Friends of the Israel Museum

Talbot, 1923; *Scheinberg*, 1975

Marionette for the Ekon society
Nigeria: Ibibio
Late 19th – early 20th century
Wood, paint
Height 58 cm
756.83

The Oron are a small group who live on the estuary of the Cross River, near the border between Nigeria and Cameroon. Although the much-larger neighboring Ibibio population claims that the Oron were merely one of the Ibibio clans, the Oron insist that they are a distinct and indigenous people.

In either case, between 1750 and 1900 the Oron created a sculptural style of great originality. Their figures of ancestors are assemblies of contrasting rectangular and spherical forms in vertical succession. The personages often wear a high, rounded headdress. Their angular chins model the generally long and plaited beards of chiefs, which they sometimes touch with one hand. They also carry regalia in the forms of horns and fans.

In earlier times, groups of these figures were kept in shrines, where offerings were made to them twice a year. Their cult, and the carving of the figures, apparently lapsed about a century ago.

Gift of Faith-dorian and Martin Wright, New York, to American Friends of the Israel Museum, in memory of Abraham Janoff

Ancestor figure (*ekpu*)
Nigeria: Oron
18th–19th century
Wood
Height 76 cm
900.84

Around the upper Benue River, a tributary of the Niger River in eastern Nigeria, there live a number of relatively small tribal groups. Among them are the Mumuye, Jukun, Wurkun, and Waja, who all use a very distinctive type of mask, which must be carried on the head rather than placed over it or worn in front of the face. Its lower part forms an inverted "U" shape; this is surmounted by a long neck and small, stylized human head. During use, the mask's lower part is largely concealed by a long fiber skirt.

Mumuye masks, the best known of the type, exhibit the usual Mumuye rounded forms, disk eyes, and large, protruding round ears, which are not present here. The rigorous angularity of the features in this example suggests its origin from another group, perhaps the Wurkun.

Gift of Jacques Kerchache and family, Paris

Shoulder mask
Nigeria, Benue River
Late 19th — early 20th century
Wood, paint
Height 163 cm
76.85

The Cameroon Grasslands

The many kingdoms of the Cameroon grassland plateaus are each governed by a ruler, his council, and a number of societies composed of the nobility and the wealthy. The Bamileke ruler, the Fon, maintains – in theory – absolute secular power as well as religious responsibility for the fertility of the land. The Mkem, his council of eight descendants of the original founders of the kingdom, advises him on matters of state. The societies each have (or, rather, had) administrative and regulatory duties, and each functioned according to a hierarchical internal structure. They met regularly at the palace in secrecy, making public appearances on occasions of great political importance, including royal funerals.

As in other African kingdoms, art in Cameroon concentrated on the needs of the court and its functions, by the creation of royal treasures and architecture. Each of the societies boasts its own rich regalia of masks, mostly carved in wood, and their accompanying costumes. The elephant mask originated among the Bamileke, and was worn by members of the Kemdje and Kuosi warrior societies. It was adopted in other Grasslands kingdoms to the north and west, namely the Bangwa and the Bamenda-Tikar.

The main element of the costume is a hood mask of cloth, covered with polychrome beadwork in geometric patterns, representing the elephant's long trunk and huge, flapping ears. To this are added various beaded and modeled cloth headpieces: a circular hat, a group of human figures, or, as in this example, a cap with the figure of a leopard. The rest of the costume is of blue and white cloth, with a leopard skin worn on the back. The beads used on these masks were imported in the nineteenth century from Venice and Czechoslovakia; to this day, they denote great wealth. Even more significant are the symbolic images of the leopard and elephant, creatures whose strengths are likened to those of the ruler himself.

Note: the two objects are not from an original ensemble.

Headpiece: Gift of Arnold and Milly Glimcher, New York, to American Friends of the Israel Museum, in memory of Joseph Lauder

Mask: Gift of Richard and Ann Solomon, New York, to American Friends of the Israel Museum

Northern, 1975

Leopard headpiece and
elephant mask
Cameroon, Southern Grasslands:
Bamileke
Late 19th – early 20th century
Cloth, beads, cowries

Headpiece: Length 1.47 cm
198.84

Mask: Height 100 cm
B95.1159

When the royal societies of the Wum or Bafum kingdoms make a ceremonial entrance, they are preceded by a running herald named Mabu. He wears a mask with harshly emphatic features and a cloak of black feathers. His function is to give warning that the members of the society are approaching, since they must not see, or be seen by, women and children during these events.

Gift of Mr. and Mrs. Charles Benenson, Greenwich, Connecticut, to American Friends of the Israel Museum

Herald's mask
Cameroon, Northern Grasslands:
Wum or Bafum
Late 19th – early 20th century
Wood, paint
Height 25 cm
744.83

Throughout the group of small kingdoms that ruled the Cameroon grasslands, wooden thrones were the most important insignia of royalty. Carved in one piece from large logs, the standard form had an open, lower ring connected by subsidiary figures to an upper disk that was the seat. Their most striking feature, however, is that they incorporate figure sculptures of varying degrees of complexity. In the kingdom of Kom, for instance, the seat is dwarfed by a life-sized statue of a past ruler, either male or female, standing behind it. The figures were completely covered in precious red and blue glass beads, with their faces sheathed in copper.

The figures on the perimeter of the present throne's seat show an entire scene. The king is seated on a low stool, wearing a decorated hat. His widespread legs are drawn up, and the elbows of his extended arms rest on his knees. His left hand is placed on the head of a small female attendant, who carries a gourd flask of palm wine; his right is on the head of a man holding the king's buffalo-horn drinking cup. The supporters of the seat, standing on the ring base, are a large leopard and two more small figures. The group of images is replete with references to royal wisdom and power: the insignia, the leopard, and the king's pose itself, which evokes the abstract motif that represents the frog and the spider — both symbols of fertility.

The royal group is virtually identical with that on a throne in the British Museum, which has a similar but more elaborate base. Collected in Bagam, south of Babanki, this was said to have been carved (more probably commissioned) by a king of Babanki-Tungo.

Gift of Jane Stern Lebell, New York, to American Friends of the Israel Museum

Throne
Cameroon, Northern Grasslands:
Bamenda-Tikar area, probably carved in
Babanki-Tungo kingdom
Late 19th – early 20th century
Wood
Height 92 cm
B00.1442

Central Africa

The Fang are today a large assemblage of related smaller groups, each with its own name. Like the Kota, they appear to have migrated at different times from a region northeast of the present country of Gabon. The date of the earliest migration is unknown, but the latest took place towards the end of the eighteenth century.

Byeri was a Fang cult of lineage ancestors that has affinities with the parallel cults of the Kota and Mahongwe. Young males were inducted into the cult by a severe and painful process of initiation, through which they became fully adult males. The ancestors – who could be either male or female – were worshiped, and their goodwill towards their descendants was solicited.

The ancestral relics (usually the skulls) were preserved in lidded cylindrical containers made of sewn-together bark sheets. Attached to their lids were either carved wooden heads, heads with arms and torsos, or full-length figures. The full-length *byeri* figures "sat," so to speak, at the edges of the reliquary boxes with their legs hanging down the sides. They were secured in place by a peg, projecting from the buttocks, that fitted inside the box. The heads were sometimes crowned with bundles of feathers. The boxes were kept in the chiefs' houses.

Half-length figure (*byeri*)
on reliquary lid
Gabon: Fang
Late 19th – early 20th century
Wood, bark, cane, brass tacks
Height 38 cm
B97.0005

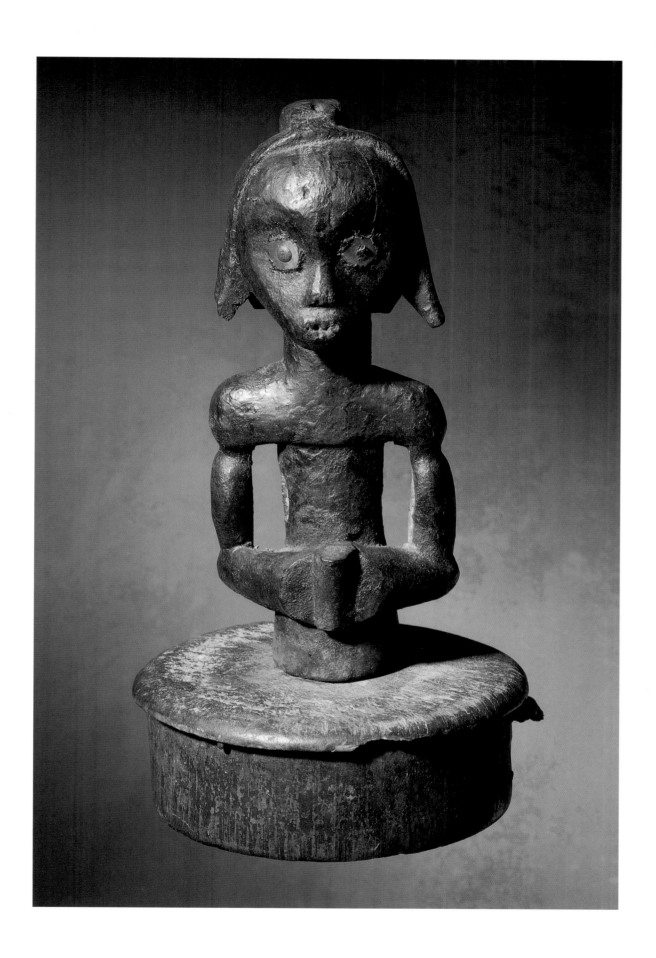

There are a number of recorded sub-styles of these *byeri* figures, usually distinguished by their hairstyles or overall proportions. They were regularly anointed with oil that gives them a wet, black sheen and, in many cases, never dries out.

The style of the female figures is typical of the sculptures of the southern Fang groups. The broad face, with its domed brow, protruding jaws, and exposed teeth, surmounts a stocky body with markedly muscular limbs; the hands are clasped in front of the torso. Since they represent females, the figures wear bracelets on the upper arm and bear incised scarification marks on the brow and under the eyes.

Female reliquary figure (*byeri*)
Gabon: Fang
Late 19th – early 20th century
Wood
Height 48 cm
B97.0071

Such figures, like the other *byeri* carvings and heads, were considered the guardians of the sacred ancestral bones. Curiously, however, they seem not to have been sacred in and of themselves. They could be seen by the uninitiated, and were even used as puppets to entertain the villagers in the final stage of funeral rites.

The two Fang-Ngumba figures shown here are representative of the northern style of Fang *byeri*. While they assume the general pose of all such figures, their features show less of the aggressive stylization of the southern figures, their musculature is less developed, and – characteristically – the necks and torsos are conspicuously elongated.

Half-length figure and female reliquary figure (B97.0071): Gift of Lawrence Gussman, Scarsdale, New York, to American Friends of the Israel Museum, in memory of Catharine R. Gussman

Female reliquary figure (B98.0055): Gift of Lawrence Gussman, Scarsdale, New York, to American Friends of the Israel Museum, in memory of Dr. Albert Schweitzer

Pair of figures: Gift of Lawrence Gussman, Scarsdale, New York, to American Friends of the Israel Museum, in memory of Dr. Albert Schweitzer and David C. Miller, and in honor of Rena Schweitzer Miller

Perrois and Sierra Delage, 1991

Female reliquary figure (*byeri*)
Gabon: Fang
Late 19th – early 20th century
Wood, brass sheet, brass tacks
Height 49.5 cm
B98.0055

Pair of reliquary figures (*byeri*)
Cameroon: Fang-Ngumba
Late 19th – early 20th century
Wood, brass sheet, mirror glass
Height: female figure 54 cm;
male figure 51.5 cm
B97.0004 (a–b)

This work belongs to a group of masks that may have one, two, or as many as six faces. As usual when the faces are multiple, one is larger than the others; the wearer sees through eyeholes in the cylindrical hood in which they are set. Each face is decorated with a different pattern, probably representing tattoos or scarification marks.

The name of the mask presents a small mystery: it apparently means "face of a young white girl." Who is this girl? Perhaps she is a visitor from the afterlife, where the spirits are white, rather than a literal reference to a European woman (although the Fang sometimes believe that their ancestors are reincarnated in the countries where the "whites" live).

In the past, the Fang dancer underwent an initiatory rite so that he became possessed by the spirit of the "white girl." Among some of the Fang, the performance was also related to the *byeri* ancestor cult. Today, dance and dancer are apparently taken less seriously, and appear at feasts as part of the celebrations.

Gift of Lawrence Gussman, Scarsdale, New York, to American Friends of the Israel Museum, in memory of Dr. Albert Schweitzer

Perrois, 1986

Four-faced helmet mask (*ngontang*)
Gabon: Fang
Early 20th century
Wood, kaolin, paint
Height 34 cm
B97.0006

Masks of this greatly elongated type apparently first appeared in Europe about 1890, approximately two decades before the society with which they were associated was banned by colonial authorities. With its suppression, much information about the society disappeared as well.

The Ngil society was widespread among the northern Fang groups and others to the southeast of them. It was dedicated to the eradication and punishment of sorcery — a function over which it attempted to maintain an undoubtedly profitable monopoly — as well as such more recondite offenses, Perrois tells us, as "stamping one's feet on the ground, contemplating the moon, [and] calling snakes by name."

It has been stressed that, though the mask (*ngel*), in its economy of form, may give an impression of serenity, this was not the intention of its makers. The mask's distortion of human features, with its arched eyebrows, lengthy nose, and tiny mouth, was deliberately intended to intimidate.

The Arthur and Madeleine Chalette Lejwa Collection, bequeathed by Madeleine Chalette Lejwa to American Friends of the Israel Museum

Perrois, 1986

Mask (*ngel*)
Gabon: Fang
Late 19th — early 20th century
Wood, kaolin, paint
Height 47 cm
B00.0898

A number of tribes known collectively as the Kota live around tributaries of the upper Ogowe River in eastern Gabon, to which they migrated from the northeast about 400 years ago. The Hongwe (or Mahongwe) live in the northeast of Gabon, and are the northernmost of these groups. Like other Kota, they traditionally practiced an ancestral cult (Bwete) that preserved the bones of important persons in basketry reliquaries topped with wooden figures covered in metal sheet and stripping.

The reliquary figures of the Hongwe, though similar in principle, depart further from naturalism than do the other Kota styles. The main element in these figures is an ogee arch, pointed at the top, from which a small projection protrudes back — perhaps representing a kind of coiffure. In spite of the figure's considerable abstraction, it is possible to discern the eyes, a forehead (shown as a copper strip), and possible mustaches on either side of the nose. On complete figures, an open, sub-circular form at the bottom may represent the arms, as is the case in the Kota figures from groups further south.

Gift of Lawrence Gussman, Scarsdale, New York, to American Friends of the Israel Museum, in memory of
Dr. Albert Schweitzer

Reliquary figure (*boho na bwete*)
Gabon: Hongwe
Late 19th – early 20th century
Wood, brass sheet and wire, iron
Height 25.5 cm
B98.0053

Living south of the Hongwe, the Shamaye make reliquaries in a different style that is related to those yet further south. The face is an oval, pointed at the top and bottom, with a tab above the head and two smaller ones on each side of the chin. A long, thin nose runs from the top of the head nearly to the chin, with close-set eyes on each side about midway down the oval. These eyes are roughly the focal point of four diagonal metal strips, which divide the surface into quadrants that are filled with metal strips parallel to the diagonals — except for the mouth and chin area, which are covered by a metal plate with repoussé designs. A slender neck connects the head to an open diamond with straight sides, repeating the angles of the diagonal strips.

The Arthur and Madeleine Chalette Lejwa Collection, bequeathed by Madeleine Chalette Lejwa to American Friends of the Israel Museum

Reliquary figure (*bwete*)
Gabon: Shamaye
Late 19th — early 20th century
Wood, brass, copper
Height 39.5 cm
B00.0662

In the area of Gabon south of the Hongwe and Shamaye, skulls and other bones of ancestors were preserved in reliquaries of bark cylinders or in plaited containers. Upon these reliquaries, too, were set flat wooden carvings of heads atop (in most cases) a transverse open diamond; the heads were transformed into faces by attached copper or brass sheets and strips. The reliquaries were housed on shelves in open-fronted shrines, usually outside the villages, and were kept carefully polished with sand to maintain their shining surfaces.

There are at least seven major styles of these heads, each including several sub-styles. This example belongs to the best-known, "classic" Kota type, made by the Obamba and Mindumu tribes in southeast Gabon. Its formal scheme is simple: two half-moons bracketing an oval face, which has a smaller arced crest above it, and an open diamond supporting a short cylindrical neck below the face. The open diamond may represent the ancestor's arms. A simple ensemble of geometrical shapes, the effect of the whole is one of great formal beauty.

Although examples of these reliquary figures were first collected by explorers, and presented to the Trocadero Museum in Paris as early as 1883, they attracted little attention for a quarter of a century. Then, owing partly to the interest contemporary artists took in them, the figures gained a place as preeminent icons of African art, which they have retained ever since.

Gift of Mr. and Mrs. Chaim Gross, New York, to American Friends of the Israel Museum

Reliquary guardian figure (*mbulu ngulu*)
Gabon: Kota
Late 19th – early 20th century
Wood, copper sheet, brass sheet
Height 58 cm
752.83

These two reliquary figures exemplify variants of a further sub-style of the Kota reliquary figures. This type is distinguished by the convexity of the faces, with their huge foreheads and ridged, horizontal eyes, and by the turned-up tips of the side panels that frame them.

The smaller piece is probably another *mbulu ngulu* from the Obamba-Mindumu groups; the larger, the *mbulu viti*, hails from the Mindassa and Bawumbu, who span the far southeast of Gabon and the northern Democratic Republic of the Congo, around the upper Ogowe River.

Formerly in the Helena Rubinstein Collection
The Arthur and Madeleine Chalette Lejwa Collection, bequeathed by Madeleine Chalette Lejwa to American Friends of the Israel Museum

Perrois, 1986

Two reliquary figures
(*mbulu ngulu, mbulu viti*)
Gabon: Kota
Late 19th – early 20th century
Wood, brass, copper
Height 38.5, 51 cm
B00.0912 (a–b)

The powerful image with which this *mbulu ngulu* presents us is another variant of the Obamba and Mindumu styles. Unlike the serene "classic" figures, this style has a dramatic, almost menacing forcefulness due to the aggressive versions of the design elements that compose it and the interplay between them. The elegance of the flat, curved upper crescent, the sweeping side panels, and the slender neck and arms contrasts with the massive bulging brow, with its strong central ridge and arched eyebrows. The lowering gaze of the pale, protruding bone eyes adds a finishing stroke of vigorous immediacy.

Gift of Lawrence Gussman, Scarsdale, New York, to American Friends of the Israel Museum, in memory of
Dr. Albert Schweitzer

Reliquary guardian figure (*mbulu ngulu*)
Gabon: Kota
Late 19th – early 20th century
Wood, copper sheet, brass sheet
and wire, iron, cranial bone
Height 53.5 cm
B98.0052

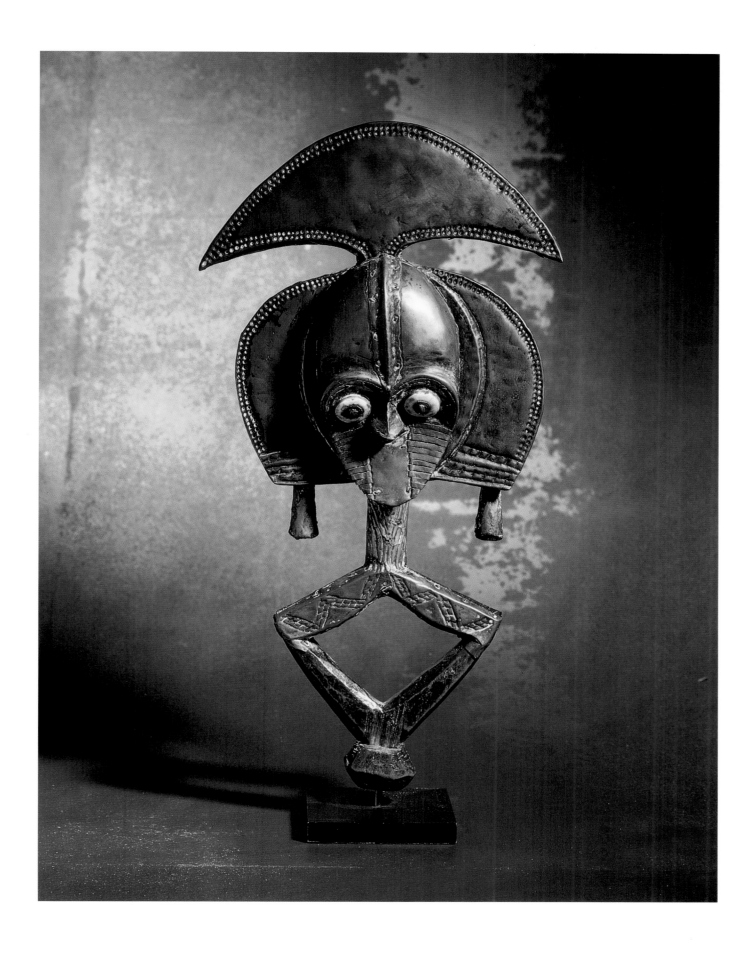

The exact origin of this rare mask is obscure, but its suggested provenance is strongly supported by the use of the Kota and Mahongwe technique – unusual elsewhere in Africa – of attaching sheet metal with prominent staples to a light wooden base. Here the method is used on a rounded, three-dimensional surface rather than the mainly flat planes of the reliquary figures.

The face of the mask takes up relatively little of the whole form. It has a bulging brow, short nose, and small, protruding mouth. These features are also consistent with those of some Kota reliquary figures. A flange runs down each side, and a crest runs from side to side above the brow, with a raised rectangular block marking the middle. It is uncertain whether the piece was actually used as a face mask at all, even though the slit eyes piercing the wood would suggest so. Unlike most functional masks, this piece has depth almost equal to its height, and very little of the wood has been removed in the back to accommodate a wearer's face. In any case, its ethnographic context is undetermined.

Very few other works of this type are known. A similar object was formerly in the Pierre Verité Collection, Paris, attributed to the Kota by William Fagg; a third was in the Paul Tishman Collection, New York. These two are practically identical in form with our example, though their details are rather more precisely defined.

Formerly in the Vincent Price Collection
Gift of Lawrence Gussman, Scarsdale, New York, to American Friends of the Israel Museum, in memory of
Dr. Albert Schweitzer

Mask
Gabon: Kota
Late 19th – early 20th century
Wood, brass sheet
Height 27.5 cm
B98.1060

Like the Kota group, the Mbete are migrants from the northeast who arrived in the area about the same time and now live a little to the east of the Kota on the border between Gabon and the Democratic Republic of the Congo. The Mbete also make carvings used as ancestral reliquaries, but of completely different form from those of the Kota and Hongwe: theirs are full-length, standing figures of the ancestors. In this aspect they are closer to the reliquary figures of the Fang. The relics are inserted into a long, vertical slot in the figure's back, which is then closed by a lid attached with ties or sealed with resin.

Although its legs are lost, this figure typifies the Mbete style in the angularity of the arms and the almost cylindrical body. The head, with its domed brow, straight nose, and deep-set eyes, shows a relationship to the faces on some types of Kota reliquary figures.

Gift of Klaus Perls, New York, to American Friends of the Israel Museum

Reliquary figure
Gabon: Mbete
Late 19th – early 20th century
Wood, paint
Height 45 cm
562.84

Although some masks of this type are known to date from the late nineteenth century, virtually nothing is known about them. They are, certainly, among the most sparingly geometric representations of the human visage in all of African art. The features are restricted to the upper third of a long, almost flat panel pointed at the lower end, or "chin," so that all that is to be seen of them is a beetling brow and a long, narrow nose, with eyes and mouth indicated only by small slits. Apart from this, the whole is painted in four red and white quadrants.

Known as efficient and well-traveled boatmen on the Ogowe River, the Aduma are credited with having disseminated some local style elements over wider ranges. Some of the metal-covered reliquary figures of the Kota and Mahongwe, for instance, show very much the same minimalist treatment of the face, while certain Fang masks are similarly divided into quadrants of contrasting colors.

Gift of Lawrence Gussman, Scarsdale, New York, to American Friends of the Israel Museum, in memory of
Dr. Albert Schweitzer

Mask (*mvudi*)
Gabon: Aduma-Mbete
Late 19th – early 20th century
Wood, paint
Height 37 cm
B97.0007

The "white masks" of southern Gabon have long been among the most famous of all African sculptures. They are carved by the Lumbo and Punu around the coast, and further inland, to the east; the Tsangui in the northern Democratic Republic of the Congo produce them in a slightly variant style.

Small in size, the masks have naturalistic human features, painted white with kaolin, framed below by a collar and above by a thick, helmetlike coiffure (described as a "bivalve" form) rising to a peak with short braids on either side. The collar and hair are painted in a contrasting black. The faces are notably delicate, with small noses and mouths and pointed chins. The most expressive features are the large, closed eyelids and strongly arched eyebrows; it is owing to these that the masks have a strikingly meditative, almost dreamy look. Some have a diamond pattern in relief on the forehead, indicating scarifications, and are therefore probably masks of women.

Worn by men at funerary rites, *okuyi* masks represented – or perhaps were even intended as portraits of – ancestors. In contrast to the stillness of the masks' appearance, the dancers' actions were vigorous. The masker wore a cloth cloak and trousers, carried whisks in each hand, and paraded through the village on short stilts, performing acrobatic feats.

Gift of Lawrence Gussman, Scarsdale, New York, to American Friends of the Israel Museum, in memory of Dr. Albert Schweitzer

Perrois, 1986

Mask (*okuyi*)
Gabon: Lumbo-Punu
Early – mid-20th century
Wood, paint, kaolin
Height 25.5 cm
B97.0008

The Kuyu, a subgroup of the Mboshi, live on the east and west banks of the Kuyu River, a tributary of the Congo. Both groups hold initiations during which the powers of certain animals are revealed. For the western Kuyu, the animal is the panther, the personification of the chief. For the easterners, it is the serpent Ebongo, shown as a carved human head mounted on a long pole, concealed by draperies and manipulated to mime the serpent's writhing. The heads are ovoid and crowned with feathers. During the initiation, the serpent is joined by male and female figures representing the primordial couple – respectively Joku and Ebotita.

Larger figures are said to depict ancestral chiefs. Their style is often remarkable for the squat proportions of the bodily configuration, emphasized by its barrel-shaped head, torso, and limb forms, and by the lack of neck. The faces, nearly as wide as the shoulders, have slit eyes, broad noses, and diamond-shaped mouths with parted lips revealing the teeth. The faces and torsos are covered with relief bands – usually rows of small squares – replicating body scarification. All these details are enhanced with vivid polychromy; the black surface of this one is exceptional. To add to the complex effect, the figures sometimes stand on other human heads, or are topped with small figures of animals – perhaps those that were taboo to certain clans. The figures appear to have been displayed at the initiation ceremonies.

Gift of Lawrence Gussman, Scarsdale, New York, to American Friends of the Israel Museum, in memory of Dr. Albert Schweitzer

Nicklin, 1983

Female figure
Democratic Republic of the Congo:
Mboshi (Kuyu)
Late 19th – early 20th century
Wood
Height 59.6 cm
B98.0058

The Kongo, who live in the territory around the mouth of the Congo River (including northern Angola), established a kingdom on its banks about the end of the fourteenth century. Already dominating the trade in ivory and other commodities, the Kongo profited greatly, with the arrival of the Portuguese in 1483, from exchanges that included slaves. These contacts grew even closer, with ambassadors from Europe presenting themselves at the Kongo king's court; when missionaries arrived, the king and other rulers became converts to Christianity. These relationships, and the kingdom itself, collapsed following a crucial battle with the Europeans in 1665.

A stone *ntadi* ("watchman") figure was placed on the grave of a Kongo chief or other distinguished person. The tradition of carving *mintadi* (plural) in soft stone may have begun about the sixteenth century, gaining impetus in the nineteenth century and coming to an end in the early twentieth century.

The figures always show an individual – in the majority of cases male, though some show a female with a child – wearing a cylindrical cap, on a plinth. Positions vary; most figures are seated cross-legged, or with one raised knee. Often the head leans on one hand or a knee, but sometimes other gestures are shown. This example is unusual: the kneeling pose with upraised hands suggests an attitude of prayer or supplication, but has also been interpreted as indicating the generosity of a ruler.

Gift of Lawrence Gussman, Scarsdale, New York, to American Friends of the Israel Museum, in honor of Sarita Gantz

Bandelier, 1968; *Cornet*, 1978

Kneeling figure (*ntadi*)
Democratic Republic of the Congo:
Kongo
16th –19th century
Steatite
Height 35.5 cm
B97.0018

As is common throughout the Congo River basin, carvings of human figures are vehicles of spiritual power among the Teke. The ruler possesses one such figure of particular strength, but others may be owned by individuals of lower status. The figures are carved with a head and legs, but frequently lack arms. The middle of the body is entirely enveloped in a coating of magic materials – including animal and plant scraps – embedded in a mass of *bonga* (kaolin). This mineral, powdery and white in its natural state, is thought of as the remains of ancestral bones. The sculptural quality of these figures derives precisely from the juxtaposition of the natural, irregular form of the kaolin mass with the carefully carved, geometric style of the head.

Gift of Jeffrey B. Soref, New York, to American Friends of the Israel Museum

Figure (*butti*)
Democratic Republic of the Congo: Teke
Late 19th – early 20th century
Wood, magical material, kaolin
Height 28 cm
167.84

The Yaka and the main group of the Suku live in adjacent areas between the Kwango and Kwilu rivers south of the Congo River. They are surrounded by smaller ethnic groups among which are scattered enclaves of minor Suku communities. Their propinquity has resulted in their sharing a number of cultural traits, including religious conceptions and art styles. Both have circumcision rituals that take place during male initiation, and experts in religious rituals who have also undergone special initiations.

As in other parts of Africa, the people's belief in the existence of a creator god does not entail a cult; it is the ancestors who are invoked in appeals for their aid in human affairs. Here, as elsewhere, carved figures are the vehicles through which such calls for intervention are made. They are carved to be the containers of protective magical power exercised by the experts against illness, to avenge sorcery, and for supernatural assistance in hunting. Small pouches containing magic materials (now often removed from collected examples) are attached to them.

Suku and Yaka sculptures show close similarities in proportion and stance. They are often mainly to be distinguished by the Yaka use of a greatly exaggerated turned-up nose, a feature sometimes said to represent the elephant's trunk. This also appears to a modified extent in Suku figures, which are marked by the very distinctive articulation of firmly defined sections of the body seen in this example. The gesture of the raised hands is said to express sorrow or mourning.

Yaka figure: Gift of Mr. and Mrs. Edwin Silver, Los Angeles, to American Friends of the Israel Museum

Suku figure: Gift of Lawrence Gussman, Scarsdale, New York, to American Friends of the Israel Museum, in honor of James Shasha

Bourgeois, 1984; *Cornet,* 1971

Female figures (*biteki*)

Democratic Republic of the Congo: Yaka
Late 19th – early 20th century
Wood, magical material
Height 36 cm
772.83

Democratic Republic of the Congo: Suku
Late 19th – early 20th century
Wood
Height 49.5 cm
B97.0011

Like other groups in the area, the Pende migrated, in fairly recent times, from Angola; they now form a large population spread out over an extensive area, which they have maintained despite invasions by the Chokwe and others. Their society is matriarchal, and divided into a number of chiefdoms.

The best-known Pende works are small masks worn at circumcision ceremonies. These *mbuya* are characterized by broad faces with rounded foreheads and arched eyebrows over heavily drooping eyelids; the lower part of the face is sharply triangular, marked by parted lips exposing the teeth. There are a number of types, often with the triple conical headdress worn by chiefs. Exquisite tiny copies of these in ivory were worn as amulets.

The *pumbu ya mfumu* ("power of the chief") mask is very different, and almost abstract: long and semi-rectangular, it has tubular eyes that project from a red-painted field, a triangular nose extending most of the height of the mask, and a small mouth. The lower part of the mask is covered with horizontal bands of alternating black and white triangles. These masks were kept in semi-secrecy, appearing only at a ceremony in which painted or carved rods were planted in the ground around a chief's house, in honor of his ancestors.

The Arthur and Madeleine Chalette Lejwa Collection, bequeathed by Madeleine Chalette Lejwa to American Friends of the Israel Museum

Sousberghe, 1958

Mask (*pumbu ya mfumu*)
Democratic Republic of the Congo,
Kasai River area: eastern Pende
Late 19th – early 20th century
Wood, paint
Height 104 cm
B00.0664

The central Democratic Republic of the Congo is inhabited by the Kuba people, who are divided into several kingdoms – the largest, and dominant, one being that of the Bushoong. The Bushoong king is said to be of divine descent: master of the natural and supernatural world, he is hailed as a being far removed from humanity. Fortunate in their geographical location, the Bushoong largely controlled the area's trade, and thereby accumulated great riches.

The Bushoong have about twenty types of masks, most of them used in initiations. Four types, however, are reserved for the sole use of the king. One of them, the *bwoom*, may only be donned by him or by those whom he nominates. In any case, the masks themselves remain royal property and must be returned to the royal treasury when the temporary "owner" dies. Each *bwoom* is given its own individual name.

As is not often the case with African art, something is actually known about the history of the *bwoom*. It appears to have been invented in the mid-eighteenth century, in a less decorated form; copper sheeting was applied later, beginning in the late nineteenth century. The mask is crowned with eagle feathers, and the costume is sumptuous. With gloves and shoes that sport attached ivory toe- and fingernails, it conceals the body completely, and is covered with dense patterns of sewn-on cowrie shells.

The word *bwoom* seems to mean "divination." As to what the *bwoom* represent, there are several different versions. One says that, like the king himself, they are forest spirits (*ngesh*). Others describe various incidents in which a past king was afflicted with madness, then cured by wearing the *bwoom*. The masks are also worn in a dance reenacting a myth of the competition of a king and a commoner for a woman.

Gift of Gaston de Havenon, New York, to American Friends of the Israel Museum

Cornet, 1982; *Vansina*, 1976

Mask (*bwoom*)
Democratic Republic of the Congo:
Kuba Bushoong
Late 19th – early 20th century
Wood, fur, copper, cloth, glass,
shells, beads
Height 50 cm
1080.79

An example of one of many types of cups, mugs, and beakers carved by the Kuba, this small wooden vessel was no doubt intended for drinking palm wine, a ritual beverage. Its fine carving is a testimony to the taste, prestige, and wealth of its former owner.

Like other Kuba cups, this high-status object refers to yet another high-status object, for it is a miniature representation of one of the tall standing drums used by the royal musicians. On its side appears a face, in typical Kuba style, joined directly to a hand. The barrel, characteristically, is covered with elegant, incised strap-work designs resembling the patterns found on Kuba textiles — or perhaps the beadwork that sheathed the royal drums.

Gift of Lawrence Gussman, Scarsdale, New York, to American Friends of the Israel Museum, in memory of Dr. Albert Schweitzer

Beaker
Democratic Republic of the Congo:
Kuba
Late 19th – early 20th century
Wood
Height 21 cm
B97.0021

The Luluwa people have had a complex and by no means happy history. Originally a large population of small hunting groups, they were beset from the early eighteenth century onward by the peoples around them. These were, first, the Luba – who took over much of their territory – then the Kuba, Pende, Chokwe, and Songye. About 1850 the Chokwe, together with Arab slave traders, organized the Luluwa into kingdoms. About twenty years later Mukenge, the ruler of one of these, succeeded in uniting most of them under his leadership. An ardent reformist, he campaigned militantly against traditional cults and the art made for them. His personal choice of religion, somewhat ahead of his time, was based on the smoking of marijuana.

In spite of this repression, and partly owing to the wealth of artistic influences to which they were nevertheless exposed, the sculpture of the Luluwa is one of the most individual of Congo styles. The works include small tobacco mortars, combs, anthropomorphic drums, and, above all, splendid commemorative figures of men, bearded and heavily armed. Smaller figures of men and women embody graceful images of considerable naturalism, their surface vitalized by relief designs representing bold patterns of keloid scarification (a fashion abolished by Mukenge in the 1880s).

Many of the small figures were used in rituals called *bwanga bwa cibola*, undertaken to procure ancestral aid, particularly in ensuring successful childbirth and guarding against children's illnesses. Often such figures are shown carrying children; the cup in this one's hand probably held magic material to be rubbed on the living child itself. The prominent herniated navel is symbolic of the connection between the ancestors and their descendants.

Gift of Lawrence Gussman, Scarsdale, New York, to American Friends of the Israel Museum, in honor of Herbert Gussman

Female figure bearing cup
(*lupingu lua luimpe*)
Democratic Republic of the Congo:
Luluwa
Late 19th – early 20th century
Wood
Height 26.5 cm
B97.0012

The Mbagani (or Binji) and Kete were groups of agricultural people who, like other indigenous Congo peoples, were largely dispersed by Luba invasions. The masks of both are notable for their concise, geometric forms. In outline, a rounded brow tapers down to a pointed chin. The relatively enormous eyes, protruding relief ovals with horizontal eye-slits, are set in rounded concave areas painted white. Between the eyes, the nose is a rectangular block; below it a smaller block forms the mouth, notched to denote the lips. The styles are related to the masks of the neighboring Lwalwa and the Salampasu.

The masks are used by the Kete in circumcision rituals. Among the Mbagani the huge eyes are associated with the ancestral spirits they worship, and the masks are worn at rites to promote successful hunting or female fertility.

Formerly in the Harold Rome Collection, New York
Gift of Lawrence Gussman, Scarsdale, New York, to American Friends of the Israel Museum, in memory of
Dr. Albert Schweitzer

Mask (*kibwabwabwa*)
Democratic Republic of the Congo:
Mbagani or Kete
Late 19th – early 20th century
Wood, kaolin, pigment
Height 28 cm
B97.0017

Minkisi (in the plural), the most important figure sculptures of the Songye, were carved in large and small versions. Both share the sculptural characteristics of bulky forms, often with sharply defined edges; domed heads, expanded noses, and rectangular beards; protruding abdomens supporting folded hands; and squat legs with large feet. The figure usually stands on a cylindrical pedestal.

Each large figure was commissioned by a chief and his council of elders. A smith then carved it, under the direction of an *nganga*, an expert in magic, for the benefit of the community as a whole. The figures were given personal names, and often became celebrated for their prowess on behalf of their people.

The basic wood carving was outfitted with attributes that denoted physical strength, supernatural power, and high status, prescribed by the *nganga*. The most significant of these was an antelope horn filled with *bishimba*, magic materials without which the figure was powerless, which was fitted on the top of the head. The same materials were also placed in a cavity in the abdomen, while other symbolic objects were hung on the limbs. When completed, the figure was a safeguard against the magic of sorcerers, and turned their evil against them.

Small figures served the same purposes for individuals and their families. These were also made with the assistance of the *nganga*, but were sometimes carved by the owner himself. Rather than serving the broader functions of the great figures, they were often employed for temporary and specific reasons: to ward off threatened sorcery attacks, to protect newborn children, or to cure bouts of illness.

Gift of Dr. Sidney and Mrs. Bernice Clyman, New York, to American Friends of the Israel Museum

Hersak, 1986

Power figure (*nkisi*)
Democratic Republic of the Congo:
Songye
Late 19th – early 20th century
Wood, horn, fur, metal
Height 57 cm
B83.0747

Luba rulers were invested with two important items of regalia: the bow stand and the scepter. Both are long wooden staffs tipped with iron and bound with copper strips. The bow stands are forked at the top into tridents that hold the weapon, surmounting the figure of a woman.

The staffs, symbolically speaking, represent oars – and are thus reminiscent of the Luba's original river habitats. The staffs also have female figures, or figures of a male and female couple, at their upper ends. The female figures commemorate, to some extent, famous women who, as founders of royal families, played an important role in the history of the Luba – and by extension, of the ruler himself. In broader terms the figures embody the essence of womanhood, with all its wisdom and fertility. Their shafts expand and contract into a series of geometric forms, triangles, and circles, engraved with abstract designs. These sections stand for the administrative center of the kingdom's capital, and the copper-bound shaft represents the savannas surrounding it and the roads leading into it.

The bow stands were not meant for public display, unlike what we generally think of as the role of royal insignia. Rather, they were housed secretively in shrines, where they were placed in the custody of a woman of high status. As highly sacred objects, these bow stands were proffered prayers and sacrifices. The scepters, on the other hand, were publicly displayed on royal occasions.

Gift of Lawrence Gussman, Scarsdale, New York, to American Friends of the Israel Museum, in memory of
Dr. Albert Schweitzer

Roberts and Roberts, 1996

Ceremonial staff (*kibango*)
Democratic Republic of the Congo,
Lualaba River area: Luba
Late 19th – early 20th century
Wood, iron, brass, beads, cord
Length 155 cm
B97.0013

Counting among the lesser Luba regalia and the paraphernalia of various religious experts were elaborate ceremonial axes. Their wooden shafts, bound with copper strips like the royal staffs, had terminals carved as female heads, complete with the Luba coiffure. The other end expanded into an oval, incised with diamond patterns; into this was set the long blade, which itself bore lateral ridges and punched designs. Such axes were often carried over the shoulder, handle forward. Besides signaling the owner's status, the axes figured in rituals connected with royalty, in which they were used to blaze the trails to be followed by initiates.

This ax type was also adopted by other peoples coming near to or under Luba influence, including the Hemba and Buyu.

Gift of Lawrence Gussman, Scarsdale, New York, to American Friends of the Israel Museum, in memory of Dr. Albert Schweitzer

Ceremonial ax (*kibiki* or *kasolwa*)
Democratic Republic of the Congo,
Lualaba River area: Luba
19th century
Wood, iron, copper
Height 32.7 cm
B98.1061

Both the Luba and the Songye who lived north of them had a type of mask called *kifwebe*, but the two were very different in form.

The Songye *kifwebe* has a domed forehead above huge eyelids and a spatulate nose. The lower part of the face is elongated, with a cubic, protruding mouth. The whole surface is covered with parallel striations infilled with paint. Male *kifwebe*s have a large crest running from front to back, while females have only a low ridge, if anything.

The Songye masks refer to a complex mythology of creation and power, whereby the details have multiple meanings. The left side of the mask represents the moon; the right side, the sun; and the striations are their rays. The nose is the tree of life; the mouth — the beak of a bird, a sorcerer's fire, or the everted lips of a forceful speaker; and the chin or beard is a symbol of wisdom and strength.

The Luba *kifwebe* was adopted from the Songye model, probably in the early years of the twentieth century. It tends to be entirely domed, with less prominent features — although the features still follow Songye conventions, and the design is worked with a similar system of concentric striations.

Unfortunately, little is known about the symbolism of the Luba masks, which may well have been as complex as that of the Songye's. Regarding their functions, we know only that they appeared in pairs at such important occasions as the death of a chief, and at rituals in honor of the ancestors.

Gift of Lawrence Gussman, Scarsdale, New York, to American Friends of the Israel Museum, in memory of
Rosaline Gussman

Hersak, 1986

Mask (*kifwebe*)
Democratic Republic of the Congo:
Luba-Hemba
Late 19th — early 20th century
Wood, pigment
Height 38 cm
B97.0015

The migrations of the Luba people led them to establish an empire in southeast Congo at the end of the sixteenth century, assimilating or expelling the indigenous groups. One of these was the Hemba, who moved eastward but eventually fell under Luba influence, especially in regard to their art.

The Hemba lived in a number of clans, each led by a chief who had virtually total control over his people. This power was reinforced by the authority he had inherited from the clan's male ancestors, who were represented by sculpted figures, the possession of which was indeed one of the chiefly attributes. On occasion, the chief would engage in ritual dialogues with the ancestors in the presence of their figures, speaking of their genealogies and his own actions, and concluding with the offering of animal sacrifices to them. Applications of the blood added to the sculptures' sleek patina.

The figures stand erect, hands folded over the lower torso. Their legs, as with other local groups, tend to a formalized shortness (they are missing here). The facial plane is more naturalistic than in Luba sculpture, where it is more acute, and the lowered eyes convey a sense of supernatural remoteness. The trim beard is a sign of masculine vitality. A distinguishing feature of Hemba figures is the coiffure, worn by both men and women, which is braided into a cruciform shape at the back.

Gift of Dr. and Mrs. Robert Kuhn, Los Angeles, to American Friends of the Israel Museum

Neyt, 1977

Ancestor figure (*singiti*)
Democratic Republic of the Congo:
Hemba
Late 19th – early 20th century
Wood
Height 53 cm
175.84

In many parts of Africa, stools are fashioned from a pair of disks; a female figure (sometimes two) stands or kneels on the lower disk to support the upper one. These stools are the property of the wealthy and aristocratic: for that reason, among others, they express in visual form important symbolic conceptions about religion and statehood. Among the Dogon, for instance, the upper disk represents the celestial realm, and the lower, the earth; the figures in between are the ancestors.

The use of female figures as stool caryatids is by no means intended to imply the subservience of women. Rather, it signifies the vital role played by women as upholders of the social order. This is notably the case among the Hemba, a matrilineal society in which, though chiefs are male, their status is transmitted through the female line. The figure in this example again shows the complex Hemba coiffure, and has a torso elaborated with the scarification patterns of the Hemba women.

Gift of Mr. and Mrs. Bernard Lewis, Los Angeles, to American Friends of the Israel Museum

Stool
Democratic Republic of the Congo
Luba-Hemba
Late 19th – early 20th century
Wood
Height 37 cm
759.83

The *so'o* mask of the Hemba is a personification of death that makes an appearance at funerals. Small and round, its deliberately grotesque features present a diametrical contrast to the noble faces of the ancestral statues. The mask represents a menacing creature – half man, half chimpanzee. Displaying an aggressively toothy grimace, it reveals itself as a being that is partly of the wild, partly of human culture. At the same time, the mask may embody and bear the name of a deceased ancestor. But in any case, it can be vengeful and ruin the crops of a person who fails to join the society that reveres it.

The *so'o* seems to operate in several other contexts. Outside of funerals, it is said, the mask can be kept in the house to ward off evil; it may also be carried by dancers on their belts. Like many spiritual beings in Africa and elsewhere, the *so'o* is ambivalent in its moods and intentions – capricious, dangerous, or possibly helpful.

Gift of Lawrence Gussman, Scarsdale, New York, to American Friends of the Israel Museum, in memory of Dr. Albert Schweitzer

Blakely and Blakely, 1987

Mask (*misi gwa so'o*)
Democratic Republic of the Congo:
Hemba
Late 19th – early 20th century
Wood
Height 23 cm
B97.0014

The Bembe are a forest-dwelling group, deriving from several others (most significantly, the Lega), that cohered about the eighteenth century. Living in small, dispersed villages that they abandoned every few years, the Bembe's basic social unit was the patrilineal clan. Governance was managed through their adoption of a simplified form of the Lega Bwami society, with far fewer grades.

The Bembe engaged in a number of cults for men and women alike; some were of ancestors, but most were of spirits associated with nature and areas of the environment. Figure sculptures, while relatively rare, were minor in scale and exquisite in execution. Some were used for healing rites; others were owned by individual Bwami members.

A number of mask types were made. The most spectacular type is the *alunga*, the embodiment of a forest spirit. A barrel-shaped helmet, the mask has janiform faces in which the features are reduced to pairs of enormous oval "eyes," with small cylindrical pupils that are sometimes framed by star shapes.

The Bembe used a distinctive type of wooden mask for one of their two modes of circumcision rites (*butende*). (No wooden masks were made for the other.) Called *emangungu*, they were donned by the recently circumcised as part of the heavy disguises they sometimes wore when they ventured out during their yearlong seclusion periods in the bush. In outline, this type is a flat plank squared off at the foot and arched at the top, where a large face is depicted. This is clearly analogous to that of the *alunga* mask: it has the same oval eye shapes (although here the eyes themselves are relief ovals), as well as a short nose and small, cylindrical mouth. The masks are rare, and it seems that the Bembe may have actually acquired them from other groups.

Gift of Lawrence Gussman, Scarsdale, New York, to American Friends of the Israel Museum, in memory of Dr. Albert Schweitzer

Biebuyck, 1972

Mask (*emangungu*)
Democratic Republic of the
Congo: Bembe
Late 19th – early 20th century
Wood, paint
Height 42 cm
B98.0056

The community of the Lega, who live in the forested, eastern part of the Democratic Republic of the Congo, is controlled by a society called Bwami, to which all men and women seek to belong. Bwami membership is organized into a hierarchical series of about six grades, admission to which is achieved through elaborate initiation ceremonies. Each grade has associated with it – among other objects, including stools, spoons, and various items of dress – certain types of small figures and masks made of wood, bone, and ivory. The masks are never designed or intended to be worn on the face, though sometimes they are placed on the upper arm. Rather, they are displayed on racks or carried in the hand by their raffia beards during the rituals to which they pertain. Masks in wood, such as this one, are part of the paraphernalia of male members of the second highest grade.

Bwami is deeply involved with the ethical aspects of life. Accordingly, each ritual object conveys exemplary stories and proverbs, expressing moral virtues or vices, which are passed on to the initiate together with the object.

Gift of Lawrence Gussman, Scarsdale, New York, to American Friends of the Israel Museum, in memory of Dr. Albert Schweitzer

Biebuyck, 1973

Mask (*lukwakongo*)
Democratic Republic of the Congo: Lega
Late 19th – early 20th century
Wood, kaolin, raffia
Height 42 cm
B97.0016

Bwami initiates also possess small figurative carvings in wood or ivory. These pieces, often quite elaborate, are symbolic of the proverbs that encapsulate the precepts and wisdom of the society, which are taught the initiates. Figures with multiple bodies and heads, for instance, often express the farsightedness that is an ideal of high-grade Bwami members. Female figures might be the property of wives of men who have attained the highest grade in Bwami, or who themselves have been initiated to the highest grade. The proverb associated with this figure is unfortunately not recorded.

Gift of Lawrence Gussman, Scarsdale, New York, to American Friends of the Israel Museum, in memory of Dr. Albert Schweitzer

Janiform female figure
Democratic Republic of the Congo: Lega
Late 19th — early 20th century
Ivory
Height 12 cm
B98.0060

Living to the north of the Democratic Republic of the Congo, the Basikasingo are among the several small groups who were overshadowed when their territory was invaded from the west and east by the Bembe and Lega, respectively. They adopted the latter's Bwami, and senior members of the society constitute the Basikasingo's effective political force.

Clan members maintain a cult of ancestors who must be appeased with offerings, especially of hunting trophies. The motives of the ancestors, who may also cause illness, are discovered through divination. The style of the figures representing them is characterized by roughly carved bodies but carefully worked faces with large eyes and prominent, bearded jaws.

Gift of Faith-dorian and Martin Wright, New York, to American Friends of the Israel Museum, in memory of Abraham Janoff

Biebuyck, 1982

Male figure (*mizi*)
Democratic Republic of the Congo:
Basikasingo
Late 19th – early 20th century
Wood
Height 56 cm
894.84

The Mangbetu originated north of their present lands, which verge on the dense equatorial forest of the northeast Democratic Republic of the Congo, an area which they usurped from its former nomadic Pygmy inhabitants to establish a settled, centralized kingdom. This was accomplished about 1860. Warlike and powerful, the Mangbetu prospered, enjoying great prestige and wealth.

Formerly, the palaces of the Mangbetu demonstrated a rare architectural sophistication, evincing great technical prowess. In these huge structures, constructed with barrel vaults supported on slender pillars, the ruler, his wives, and the court would assemble. The major efforts of Mangbetu artists were, in fact, devoted to enhancing the splendor of the court through the production of entirely secular luxury objects in wood, ivory, metal, pottery, and bark-cloth. Unlike that of almost any other African society, Mangbetu art had no religious content. It is even likely that the human image was used rarely, if ever, prior to the early twentieth century, when it became prevalent in response to the tastes – and requests – of European collectors.

This box for small valuables is of a type that was used frequently. The container is a composite of four sections. The lowest is a wooden base modeled after a woman's stool; on this stands a bark cylindrical container, the bark lid of which is surmounted by a woman's head carved in wood. The backward extension of the cranium reflects the Mangbetu custom of binding the skull in infancy to elongate it and the coiffure that was worn to stress the form.

Gift of Mr. and Mrs. Samuel Dubiner, Ramat Gan

Bastin, 1982; *Schildkrout and Keim*, 1990

Box
Democratic Republic of the Congo:
Mangbetu
Late 19th – early 20th century
Wood, bark, paint
Height 44 cm
2091.66

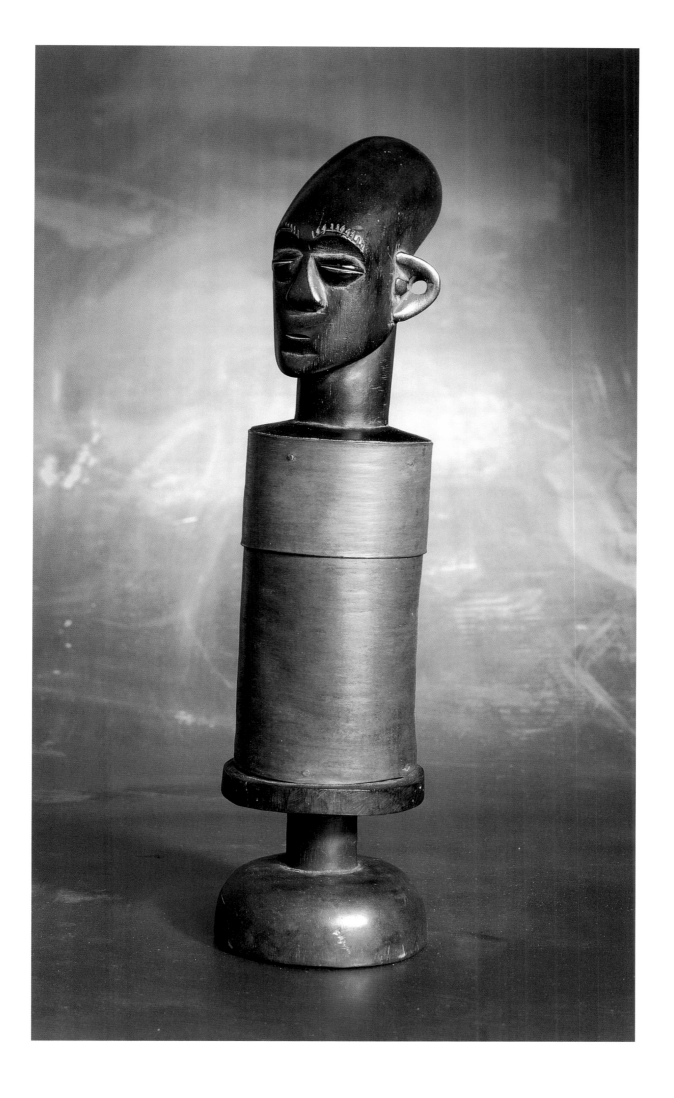

Like the Mangbetu, the Zande were invaders from the north who also established their sovereignty over a large region. Although they were frequently at war with the Mangbetu, the two cultures had much in common, including their aggression, their architecture, and aspects of their art.

Some of the better-known sculptures of the Zande are small figures (*yanda*) made for the Mani society, which was intended to promote the well-being of its members. Its dominion included their health, prosperity, safety from sorcery, and general success. The *yanda* are mainly of wood, though pottery was also used, and exist in several types. The *nazeze* are human figures, usually armless, with the large heads, trunks, and stumps of legs abstracted into geometrical forms. They were often decorated with glass beads and brass rings. Although the figures were apparently meant to represent females, they often suggest (as in this example) a markedly phallic appearance.

Gift of Lawrence Gussman, Scarsdale, New York, to American Friends of the Israel Museum, in memory of
Dr. Albert Schweitzer

Schildkrout and Keim, 1990

Female figure (*yanda, nazeze* type)
Democratic Republic of the Congo:
Zande
Late 19th – early 20th century
Wood
Height 24.5 cm
B98.0061

As a people, the Lwena originated in the sixteenth century, when a brother of a Lunda queen, following a dispute over the royal authority arising from her marriage to a Chokwe, migrated from Angola and established his own state. Living in a group of chiefdoms, the Lwena are a matriarchal society, in which both men and women can be chiefs.

Given the importance of women in their society, it is hardly surprising that Lwena figure sculpture mainly consists of small standing female figures, representing female ancestors or spirit guardians. When they are shown as pregnant, or holding a baby, they evidently are linked to the quest for fertility.

The present figure shows a graceful torso with small conical breasts and a narrow waist, the slender, right-angled arms holding a full-face image of a baby before her, just above the engraved pubic scarifications. In contrast to the upper body, the buttocks, bent legs, and feet are sturdy, even massive. The head demonstrates the strong influence of Chokwe sculpture on Lwena art, in spite of the often-hostile relations with the Chokwe which resulted in Lwena migrations to the Democratic Republic of the Congo and to Zambia about a century ago. This influence is evident in Lwena chairs following Chokwe models, anthropomorphic pottery, and the facial conventions of masks. Here the broad, almost flattened, face with its sunken elliptical eyes and summary other features, is clearly based on Chokwe models, as is the shallow, disk-shaped cap.

Formerly in the Ernst Anspach Collection
Gift of Lawrence Gussman, Scarsdale, New York, to American Friends of the Israel Museum, in memory of Dr. Albert Schweitzer

Bastin, 1969

Figure of mother and child
Democratic Republic of the Congo,
Angola, and Zambia: Lwena
Late 19th – early 20th century
Wood
Height 22.3 cm
B98.0059

East and South Africa

The southern Sudan is an expanse of savanna about half the size of France, through which flow the tributary rivers that unite to form the White Nile. At the heart of it is the huge swamp called As Sudd, around whose verges live a number of peoples, including the 3,000,000 Dinka.

During the rainy season the Dinka live in forest villages as settled agriculturalists. When the dry season comes they spend the months driving their humped, long-horned cattle from one temporary camp to another. Cattle are the mainspring of Dinka life: they constitute wealth, political power, the sources of milk and fresh blood to eat, and in a real sense, alter egos with which their Dinka owners identify themselves.

Not surprisingly, the Dinka make small clay models of cattle, which are their only visual art form beyond their treatment of their own bodies. While the Dinka traditionally go unclothed, they adorn themselves with spectacular ornamentation. Apart from ivory pendants and bracelets, their adornments consist mainly of beadwork.

Following initiation, in which horizontal scars are carved into their foreheads, young men are strapped into tight bead corsets. The colors of the beads indicate the men's status in groups organized by age. Young women, on reaching marriageable age, assume loose upper-body shirt-like garments of looped strings of blue or red beads. These signify the wealth of their families, and also the number of cattle that are expected to be paid by men who wish to become their husbands.

Woman's garment:
Gift of the Faith-dorian and Martin Wright Family, New York, to American Friends of the Israel Museum, and with the help of gifts from Armand-Pierre Arman, New York, and the Arthur and Madeleine Chalette Lejwa Collection, bequeathed by Madeleine Chalette Lejwa to American Friends of the Israel Museum

Man's garment:
Gift of the Faith-dorian and Martin Wright Family, New York, to American Friends of the Israel Museum

Woman's garment
The Sudan: Dinka
Late 19th – early 20th century
Glass beads, leather, fur, string
Height 70 cm
B00.1441

Man's garment
The Sudan: Dinka
Late 19th – early 20th century
Glass beads, leather, metal, string
Height 70 cm
B00.1699

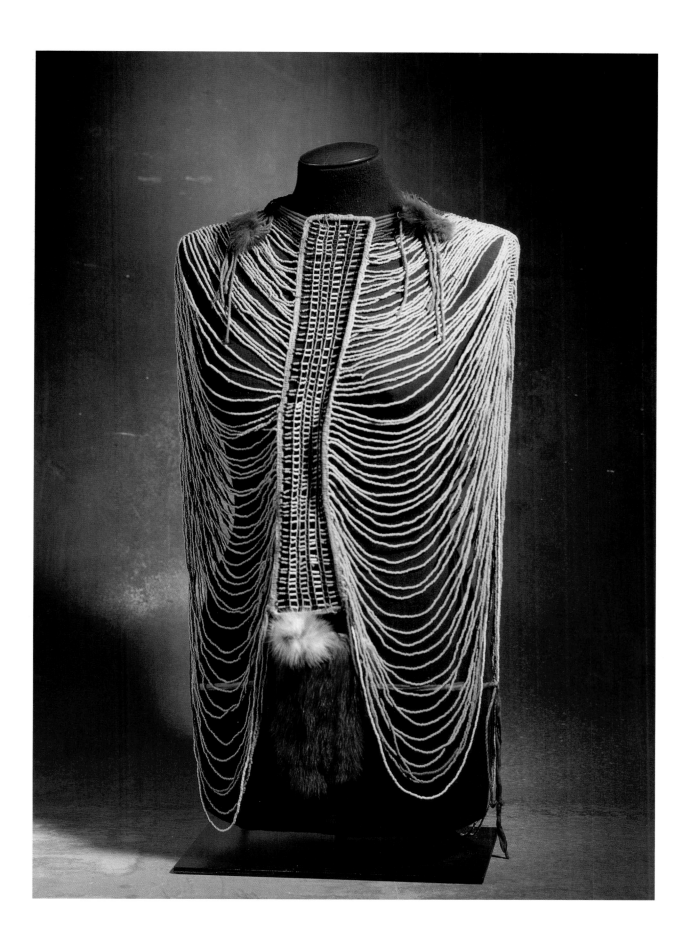

The Konso are a people in the remote south of Ethiopia. Their culture and sculpture had affinities with those of the Mijikenda of Kenya further south. Like them, they made carved figures for important deceased males; however, these figures were grave markers rather than purely memorials.

Konso males were organized into a system of age grades, the highest one known as Gada, which was responsible for promoting human and agricultural fertility. The grave markers were set up for the greater figures of the system – men who had accumulated wealth, been successful hunters, and killed enemies. Erected around his burial site, the large figures represented the dead man himself; smaller effigies commemorated his wives and the animals and human enemies he had slain. The skulls of his hunting trophies were laid at the figures' feet.

Konso figures are somewhat more naturalistic in their features and limb details than those of the Mijikenda. In general form, they seem to allude to a phallic cult. The bracelets carved in relief on the arms indicate high rank; where it occurs, a protrusion above the forehead represents the ornament assumed on attainment of Gada rank.

Gift of the Nash Family Foundation, Inc., and the Faith-dorian and Martin Wright Family, New York,
to American Friends of the Israel Museum

Grave marker (*waaga*)
Ethiopia: Konso
Late 18th – early 19th century
Wood
Height 124 cm
B95.1160

The Mijikenda are a group of agricultural peoples – including the Giryama, Chonyi, and several others – living in the hilly areas behind the coast of Kenya, to which they immigrated from Somalia in the seventeenth century. All share very similar institutions and art styles.

The Giryama are governed by a man's society called Gohu, which maintains communication between the living and the dead. Membership in the society entitles a man to have a tall, slender carved post, or *kigango*, erected in his memory. It is painted red, black, and white, "dressed" in cloth, and decorated with incised designs inlaid with plaster (which is generally lost owing to the effects of weather). The *kigango* operates as a medium through which the deceased man can be contacted and appeased if his spirit shows signs of ill will. Should a family move away, the post is left behind; but if the ancestor is well remembered, the *kigango* may be replicated in a small version, called *kibao*, set up at the new site.

The curious discrepancy between the austerely patterned plank and the representational head it sometimes supports (often the head is no more than a flat disk with coins for eyes) is actually due to a double strategy of naturalism. The head is intended to be a realistic representation of the man as he looked in life. The decorative patterning is intended to be equally realistic, as it copies that of the clothes the man wore in his lifetime.

Gift of Faith-dorian and Martin Wright, New York, to American Friends of the Israel Museum, in memory of Abraham Janoff

Wolfe, 1979

Memorial figure (*kigango*)
Kenya: Mijikenda, Giryama group
Late 19th – early 20th century
Wood
Height 185 cm
901.84

The Barotse are a confederacy of about twenty-five tribal groups who inhabit the flood plain of the Zambesi River and exercise wide influence beyond it. The Lozi are the dominant group; like the others, they are governed by a hierarchy of aristocrats.

In the past, the Lozi conducted frequent raids on surrounding peoples to obtain captives who, adopted into their society, became additional sources of manpower. They themselves were not practitioners of the arts, but employed others to make their carved and decorated objects, the most striking of which are the food bowls made by their Kwanga or Mbunda subjects. Prestige items for the aristocracy, the bowls are simple oval forms with fitted lids decorated with figures of humans or animals, including elephants, in the round. Usually, the figures are elementary and somewhat geometric. In this case, a pair of ducks swimming in line (an image found in other examples) is carved with exceptional subtlety and grace.

Gift of Lawrence Gussman, Scarsdale, New York, to American Friends of the Israel Museum, in memory of Dr. Albert Schweitzer

Lidded food bowl
Zambia: Kwanga or Mbunda,
for Lozi (Barotse)
Late 19th – early 20th century
Wood
Length 33 cm
B97.0010

In comparison with West and Central Africa, the south and east of the continent are, on the whole, considerably less prolific in sculpture. The exception occurs among the Makonde people, who are immigrants from the western hinterland now living toward the coast. Their helmet masks are basically naturalistic, but with exaggerated, heavy features: large eyes, broad flattened noses, and thick lips. Other masks for the face are delicately stylized animal heads.

This elegant little figure may have come from the top of a diviner's staff. Such objects often display the delicate carving seen here, with its typically Makonde head and precisely delineated scarification.

Gift of Mr. and Mrs. Samuel Dubiner, Ramat Gan

Female figure
Southern Tanzania –
Northern Mozambique: Makonde
Late 19th – early 20th century
Wood, paint, feathers, beads
Height 22 cm
1112.2.56

The oldest images drawn on stone surfaces in southern Africa were found in a rock shelter in Namibia. They date from 27,500 to 25,000 BCE, and are thus contemporary with the Paleolithic cave paintings of Europe. Rock engravings from later periods (10,000 and 4,000 BCE) have also been discovered. The best-known tradition of rock painting is that of the San, nomadic hunter-gatherers who live in Namibia, Botswana, and South Africa. This came to a halt with the encroachments of white settlers and others in the late nineteenth century, but had previously been vigorous and prolific. San rock painting excelled in the depiction of extensive scenes, painted in a delicate and naturalistic style, that featured mostly small images of human beings and animals. Far from being just the simple imagery of the natural life around the San they might seem, the paintings are evocative of religious and magical life.

In this fragment, one can trace part of the figure of an unknown animal and a clear figure of an eland, the antelope most often shown in the paintings. The San believed in supernatural powers that pervaded the world, and that were most fully present in this large and imposing creature. Painting on the rock, they believed, brought its immanent supernatural powers to its surface.

The work of manipulating these powers was performed by shamans who put themselves into trances. By so doing, they could communicate with the supernatural powers and obtain their aid. The eland, for example, was associated with rain, symbolized by its blood. By obtaining a vision of killing – and thus shedding the blood of – an eland, while he was in a trance state, the shaman promoted rainfall and the fertility it brought to the San's dry territory.

By exchange with the South African Museum, Cape Town, South Africa

Lewis-Williams, 1985

Rock painting
Namibia: San
Probably 18th–19th century
Stone, pigment
Length 70 cm
738.9.60

Madagascar

Madagascar, the fourth largest island in the world, lies off the east coast of Africa, 300 kilometers from the mainland. Inhabited for only the last 2,000 years, Madagascar hosts a blend of ancestral African and Indonesian populations. Indonesians apparently achieved the crossing of the Indian Ocean about a thousand years ago. Although they may have arrived initially in small numbers, they eventually became the dominating influence on the island's cultures and languages. About twenty distinct ethnic groups now exist throughout the island; their cultures show variations, but their languages are mutually intelligible.

The Mahafaly ("Joyful People") live in the arid southwestern coastal area of Madagascar, where they raise great herds of the cattle — with humps, dewlaps, and longhorns — known as zebu. As with other Madagascan groups, the celebration of the dead is a main concern. Chiefs and royal personages are buried in tombs consisting of large rectangular platforms walled with stone blocks. The skulls of oxen sacrificed during the funerals are laid on the platforms, which are further marked by tall carved posts set upon them.

The Mahafaly posts conform to a standard pattern. At the foot is a small figure, male or female, carved in the round. This is crowned by a flat panel showing a sequence of about seven or eight alternating hexagons and pairs of everted crescents, topped by a ring. Above this is a small platform on which stand carvings in the round of a zebu — sometimes with human attendants — or a pair of birds. The circle and crescents represent phases of the moon. The birds may signify the return of the soul to a regular resting place, as birds to their nests.

The stone enclosures, cattle sacrifices, and carvings all clearly derive from Indonesia and southeast Asia, where such objects are frequently linked to ritual, particularly mortuary rites, in the tribal societies. They thus exemplify the remarkable ties between Asia and Africa that Madagascar evinces.

Gift of Mr. and Mrs. C. T. Shipman, Toorak, Australia

Mack, 1986

Funerary monument (*aloalo*)
Madagascar: Mahafaly
Late 19th – early 20th century
Wood
Height 156 cm
B96.0600

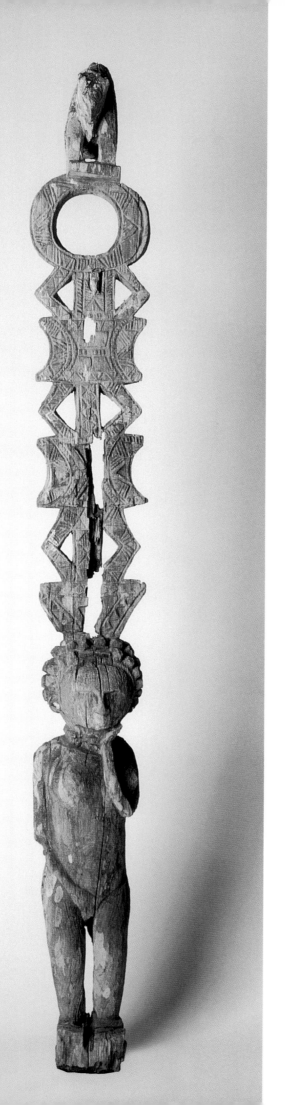

Besides the Mahafaly, several other peoples of southwest Madagascar carve monuments showing figures standing on posts (from which, as in this case, they have often been removed). These include the Vezo, Bara, and perhaps the Sakalava.

Unfortunately, the distribution of these styles of sculpture remains unclear, but this suave image of a woman shows strong similarities to examples from the Bara and, possibly, the Vezo. Among the Bara such monuments are not placed on the great tombs in the manner of the Mahafaly, but at individual sites away from the villages. Female figures are said to memorialize men.

Gift of Philippe Guimiot, Brussels, in honor of Martin Wright

Figure
Madagascar
Late 19th – early 20th century
Wood
Height 116 cm
B98.0009

Oceania

Introduction

Geography and History

Of all the waters that surround the land masses of the globe, the greatest is the Pacific Ocean, which occupies a third of the world's surface. Its eastern border is well defined, by the coasts of the Americas which run north to south, from the Bering Strait to the Strait of Magellan – nearly all the way between the polar ice caps. The western coast is less well defined by geographic terminology. Off the coasts of Asia several seas are designated separately as the Arafura Sea, the China Sea, the Timor Sea. They embrace marginal areas, including Taiwan and the nearby island of Yami, and the Philippine Islands. Nevertheless their waters are continuous with the Ocean's and, in truth, are lesser parts of it.

From the southeast of the Asian continent there extends the great Indonesian archipelago, including the large islands of Borneo and Sulawesi. Beyond these islands the Pacific Ocean itself begins. In its southwest is the continent of Australia, with the huge island of New Guinea to the north. East and north of them are the island groups collectively known as Micronesia and Melanesia. East again, towards the center of the Pacific and mainly south of the Equator, is the vast triangular area of the Polynesian islands. All these islands, then, are in the realm we call Oceania.

But is Oceania a unitary concept in human terms? Consider that Indonesia alone consists of about 14,000 islands; the other Pacific groups, about 10,000 – the great majority mere specks of coral or rock and uninhabited. Indeed, even today the population of the Pacific Ocean's islands amounts only to about 9 million people. Estimates of pre-Western populations in Oceania can hardly ever be more than conjecture, but it is clear that they were never of great size.

The Indonesian islands of Java, with its 90 million people, and Bali, respectively Muslim and Hindu, are (or rather were) the furthest outposts of the cultural and religious tides that swept out of Asia; however, it is the islands in which far different earlier customs and beliefs obtained in the past – and to a certain extent still survive – that concern us here.

Within the languages of these islands there exist three areas of commonality, even though within the groups themselves they are mostly mutually unintelligible. The languages of the Australian Aborigines are confined to the continent. There are two other great and widespread families of languages. The Papuan languages (about 800) are found in New Guinea, parts of Melanesia, and some of the Indonesian islands. The 500 Austronesian languages are distributed over a more extensive space than any other group of languages in the world. It includes Madagascar, parts of southeast Asia – hence our inclusion here of Vietnam and the Philippines – Indonesia, Melanesia, and all of Polynesia.

If one is to account for the origins of the cultures of Oceania, one must stress two facts: one is a geological event, the other a human quality. The event is the last phase of the Ice Age. Its frozen world drew back even the oceans into its grip; the seas receded even around the Equator, to expose such vast areas that in southeast Asia the present-day islands of Borneo, the Philippines, Java, and Bali were on a mainland now known as Sunda.

Archaic humans, followed by *Homo sapiens*, our own tribe, had been living in Sunda for a million years, and those who lived on the coast must have known the ways of the sea, its hazards and its possibilities, very well. The human quality that urged them on was the spirit of adventure. They began to travel, probably on bamboo rafts, to the peaks of islands that they could see to the east. They did not know it, but out there was a vast continent, Sahul, that then united what are today called the islands of Tasmania and New Guinea with Australia. Moving through the chains of islands, they reached Sahul and settled there, probably first all in Australia, about 60,000 years ago. Subsequently the pace of expansion was leisurely. People arrived in some of the great islands, to the east again, today parts of Melanesia – New Britain, New Ireland – about 30,000 years ago. These people seem to have lived by hunting, gathering wild foods, and a little cultivation of domestic plants. In some of the islands, notably New Guinea, agriculture is thought to have begun about 9,000 years ago.

Finally, about 8,000 years ago, the Ice Age released its grip; the sea waters rose, reducing the size of the islands and dividing former land masses. When the waters reached their limits, the outlines of the map of southeast Asia and its extensions of the archipelago of Indonesia, of Australia and New Guinea, and of all the islands further east then became what we see in the pages of our atlases today.

This did not mean a halt to human travel across the seas, which in fact had perhaps always continued for the sake of trade, even if only over short stages. Now it took on different forms: the development of improved seagoing vessels with a wide sailing range ultimately allowed an increased spread of populations from southeast Asia deeper into the Pacific. People of Asian descent, and probably speakers of the Austronesian family of languages, they reached Micronesia about 6,000 years ago; skirting New Guinea and Australia, they came to the islands of Melanesia, including its remoter islands of the Solomons, Vanuatu, and New Caledonia, where their languages took root. Eventually they reached the present islands of western Polynesia, Tonga, Fiji, and Samoa. Here, about 4,000 to 2,000 years ago, the distinctive culture they had brought with them developed further, and they later carried it eastwards into distant Polynesia.

The Austronesian tribal cultures of eastern Indonesia perhaps, after a long interval of time and many internal developments, can no longer be thought of as directly ancestral to those of further Oceania. Nevertheless certain of their social and religious forms have remained quite similar to those of their island cousins. It seems very probable that, at periods most of which cannot at this point be accurately defined, they not only introduced plants and animals, including the pig, but influenced in many ways the islanders' mythology, rituals, and arts.

People and Cultures

A cursory history compressed into a few sentences, such as these, might suggest a homogeneity which does not actually exist. But there are indeed aspects of the Oceanic cultures that it seems possible to trace, if only in fitful occurrences, across the Pacific Ocean, so that a few generalizations can be made about them. Even so, within the major groupings of islands, even from island to island, there are great, very striking differences, such that any summary description can only be highly impressionistic.

Throughout Oceania, natural resources inevitably determined the people's economies, and the resources were dictated by the natural scene. This ranged from desert to jungle, from high mountains to swampy lowlands, from huge tracts of land to atolls that were practically little but beaches. Thus there were people who were nomadic hunters and gatherers; who lived in settled communities, combining hunting and gathering with small-scale horticulture; others who engaged in intensive agriculture; and some who were oriented to the sea and fishing, often in different degrees and combinations. Being mostly small, the cultures developed great local diversity. Their arts are correspondingly diverse in sheer numbers of styles. Isolation accounted for the variations that existed between many cultures; so, when contacts could take place among them, did the resulting cross-fertilization.

One can say that the Australian Aborigines remained largely in isolation throughout their long history, apart from contacts on Australia's north coast with the people of the islands in the Torres Strait between Australia and New Guinea, and of southern New Guinea itself. More recently they were visited by Indonesian traders and fishermen. It seems doubtful, though, that the effects of these contacts penetrated very far into the vast hinterland.

Since the Aborigines were largely nomadic, their material equipment was limited but ingeniously adapted to their needs; everything had be easily portable and, if possible, multipurpose. Spears, spear-throwers, boomerangs, bowls that could also be used as cradles – were the modest essentials. Yet their social life was highly complex. Their religions, mainly concerned with creation and fertility, were expressed through a rich heritage of myth, song, and elaborate ritual that necessitated the creation of paintings on rock walls and bark, earth sculptures, wood carvings, and body decoration.

Down to modern times, the New Guinea cultures were, broadly speaking, classless and without hereditary leaders except where they had been touched by Austronesian influences. Individual men achieved power by force of personality and accumulation of wealth. Almost all the many cultural groups were sedentary and village-based. Religious life was largely, though not entirely, restricted to men. It often consisted of a series of initiation ceremonies which began at puberty and continued for a lifetime, each revealing further religious secrets. These involved cults of ancestral spirits and natural forces, and performance of the rituals was often accompanied by head-hunting and cannibalism, beyond the warfare that was endemic throughout the island.

Cult life, the mainspring of New Guinea arts, was centered on ceremonial houses, often grandiose in scale and sometimes lavishly decorated with paintings and sculpture, that housed sacred musical instruments, carved figures, and masks. Local styles were of an almost bewildering variety and great invention.

The same situation obtained to a great extent in the large Melanesian islands: the Admiralty Islands, New Ireland, New Britain, the Solomon Islands, Vanuatu (the islands formerly called the New Hebrides), and New Caledonia. Each of the groups had its own repertoire of styles in life and art – from the chieftainships of New Caledonia to the competitive grade societies of Vanuatu, from the complexity of New Ireland's assembled sculptures to the relative simplicity of the Solomon Islands. There are even great contrasts in the use of color, as between the stress on black in New Caledonia and the Solomons, and the rich polychrome of New Ireland and Vanuatu.

Micronesian and Polynesian societies, like those of Indonesia, were based on hierarchies of gods and human beings. The highest gods were the creators of the natural world and humanity, and were celebrated on sacred sites, often stone-built. Lesser gods governed skills and other activities. Similarly, rulers or chiefs, who in some cases approached divinity, were the highest of human beings. Often leadership was divided between the secular chiefs and high priests who governed spiritual affairs. Below them in rank were the specialized craftsmen; the lowest rank consisted of slaves, people who had lost social status for various reasons, or prisoners.

The most impressive works of art created by people of the Polynesian island groups were sculptures in wood and, rather rarely, stone – among which the huge statues of Easter Island are world-famous. Painting on flat surfaces was practically unknown, except on tapa – bark-cloth used for clothing – which was also sometimes decorated with stamped or stenciled designs. In contrast to the often flamboyant styles of New Guinea and Melanesia, though stylistically varied, Polynesian art tended to be austere and elegant, with broad, smooth surfaces. Exceptions were, for instance, the carvings of the Austral Islands that were covered in geometric designs, and the massed curvilinear designs of New Zealand Maori sculpture.

Micronesian art includes very little sculpture, except from the relatively large island of Belau (formerly Palau), where female figures in the round, and rafters carved with narrative reliefs, were incorporated into ceremonial houses that were the most impressive buildings in the whole area. Small carvings for canoe prows, charms, and masks from the Mortlock Islands are otherwise the most notable works. In the eastern Micronesian islands there was a development of fine textiles woven from banana and hibiscus fiber on back-strap looms, a technique imported from southeast Asia. These, like the wealth of ornaments, express the simplicity and supreme elegance that characterize Micronesian art.

People and Their Arts

Everywhere in Oceania that the arts flourished, it was in almost every medium. The makers were experts, who often learned their skills from their parents, generation after generation, and who were recognized, esteemed, and criticized by their communities. And although we know only few of their names, they were familiar to their contemporaries: our ignorance does not mean that they were anonymous. Sometimes the artist was a chief or at least a man of high rank, and even semi-sacred, as among the New Zealand Maori. Quite often the inception of his work was a vision or dream inspired by the use of hallucinogens or physical ordeals.

The artists used every material, permanent or ephemeral, that they could find, from wood and stone to leaves and flowers. Even the human body became a field for artistic creation, not only by personal decoration and temporary painting, but by the permanent, and very painful, procedures of skin-cutting and tattooing.

The durability of materials has always been the determining factor that has caught some of the relics of the past in the net of time. Those materials that could not last under the assaults of age and climate have disappeared: but we should bear in mind that they once existed. It is ironic that the thousands of ivory carvings and the innumerable paintings that have come down to us from the remoteness of the Paleolithic West often outnumber what has survived from many of the far more recent cultures of Oceania. Given other historical circumstances, nothing at all might have lasted in view of the use as their media of ephemeral materials, to which nature is not kind in the tropical climates. Wood, bark, tapa, and paint disappear rapidly, and tattooing lasts no longer than the skin that bore it. Consequently, by far the greater part of what now remains to us is no older than the periods following the late eighteenth century, when Western colonialism embarked on its most strenuous phase of expansion.

Oceania and the West

Western reactions to Oceanic art have passed through several phases. At a time when it was unknown to the Western world, some of the early explorers in the late eighteenth century were impressed by the skill and beauty of Polynesian carving. Not so the missionaries who followed on the explorers' tracks; they saw it mainly as the expression of savagery and idolatry, and destroyed all they could. Much of the pathetically small amount of Polynesian art that still exists (apart from the art of the New Zealand Maori) was retained only as evidence for the need of missionary endeavor.

A century later, a rise in scientific interest about exotic peoples paralleled the spread of exploration and colonial activity through the rest of the Pacific. Anthropology was becoming an established field of learning. Great collections were made as records of cultures believed to be dying, as their creators themselves were thought to be in peril of simultaneous physical extinction. The scientists who made collections were not very concerned with artistic values as such; they were not even convinced that works of art existed among the peoples they studied. Their assumptions about the cultures (always of a complexity of which, in truth, they knew practically nothing) included misapplied notions of evolutionary theory, and led to some absurd conclusions. Among the worst was that as the cultures themselves were thought to exemplify the "childhood" of humanity, their art could be compared to children's art.

How then have we seen these works, so often deeply foreign in their expression to our conceptions of art? Some might ask, Are they even works of art? – which leads us to the question, What indeed is art?

Nobody has ever given a satisfactory answer. But let us assume as an arbitrary suggestion – and it is not an original one – that art is the unnecessary elaboration of a material object that needs no such treatment. While religion was a vital impulse, and in many cultures Oceanic artists elaborated its rituals to the highest degree with the works they created to accompany it, at the same time their artistry was also employed for secular purposes and gave visual enrichment to their daily lives. None of this was strictly necessary. Many religious concepts call for no visual expression at all; and a functional implement is just as efficacious unadorned. Consequently, in some Oceanic cultures – in Micronesia, for instance – there are no ambitious or spectacular forms. But works from these cultures are often precisely the demonstration that the aesthetic sense is universal, since we find in the simplest objects an appreciation of skill, taste, and refinement.

Westerners are hardly able to look at Oceanic works of art except in the terms and modes of appreciation with which our own culture has accustomed us, to which one might say our culture has trained us. Although we can take it for granted that the artists and their audiences were susceptible to a sense of beauty, we simply do not know how it was stimulated and in what way it was felt. It has often been said that as no words existed for "art" in Oceanic languages, there must have been no conception of "art" (and therefore art did not exist).

This premise is mistaken: there are certainly terms in Oceanic languages that correspond to "artist," usually stressing gradations of knowledge and ability. Art, say the Kilenge of New Britain, is what is "well made." An aesthetic vocabulary did exist in many places, perhaps in all if we only knew them. To take a well-known example: the Maori artist's work was intended to produce *wehi* (awe or fear), and convey *ihi* (power) and *wana* (authority). These expressions may not correspond to ours, but they do give us an inkling of certain associations concerning works of art. The affective balances of Oceanic art may not be the same as ours, but they were very powerful in the cultures.

A revolutionary change of opinion took place soon after the turn of the twentieth century, when several young European artists, mainly in France and Germany, found in pieces of African sculpture resonances of form and spirit with their own work. The sympathy is understandable because much African sculpture does share, not so much the appearances, but certainly the underlying formal canons that have always existed in Western art. An equivalent attraction to the art of Oceania, the native Americas, and Indonesia was discovered some twenty years later by the Surrealist artists. They have perhaps been given too much credit for this. Commercial collectors, apart from the scientists, had been busily at work in

Melanesia since at the latest the 1880s, leading to the formation of private collections; and several exhibitions had been held since 1900. The artists' knowledge of what they were seeing and the meanings they read into it remained as uninformed as ever: but they rightly stressed its magic and emotional power.

A great deal has been said and written about the effects of African and Oceanic arts upon modern Western artists, and those effects have been highly exaggerated. They have certainly not lasted into the present day. On the other hand, the infection of the artists' enthusiasm helped bring these arts before a wide Western public. Africa, Oceania, Indonesia — these began to become part of a general consciousness that a large, unfamiliar segment of the world was also deeply concerned with the visual arts.

In the last few decades, the scene has changed again, in two major ways. A great deal of research has been carried out on these arts and the cultures that created them — an essential task, as indeed they are now at last changing radically under the modern world's global impact. It is largely due to these inquiries, in fact, that it has been possible to write the explanatory texts in this book. At the same time, libraries of illustrated books have been published, and numerous exhibitions held. Access to Oceanic art is easier than ever before, and the works themselves are increasingly finding the representation they rightly merit in a wider world's aesthetic judgments.

Present and Future

Nor is their story ended. The scene of art production in Oceania is now as complex as it has ever been. A good deal is being produced along traditional lines, some of it in revivals that are energized by a drive for cultural revitalization intended to support ideals of pride in self and ethnic identity. Other work of the kind is done for commercial reasons, as products that will generate income on the market. With this there come new blends of traditional iconography and themes.

There are artists who have broken away from traditional modes altogether, and are experimenting with new media (including metal, collage, and oil painting) and the international styles of the twentieth century. Usually working in urban settings, like their Western peers, some of them have gained international reputations. It is also an important sign of change that many talented women are now entering fields of art that were previously confined strictly to men. Where all these old and new modes will lead the contemporary artists of Oceania we can only wait to see.

Douglas Newton

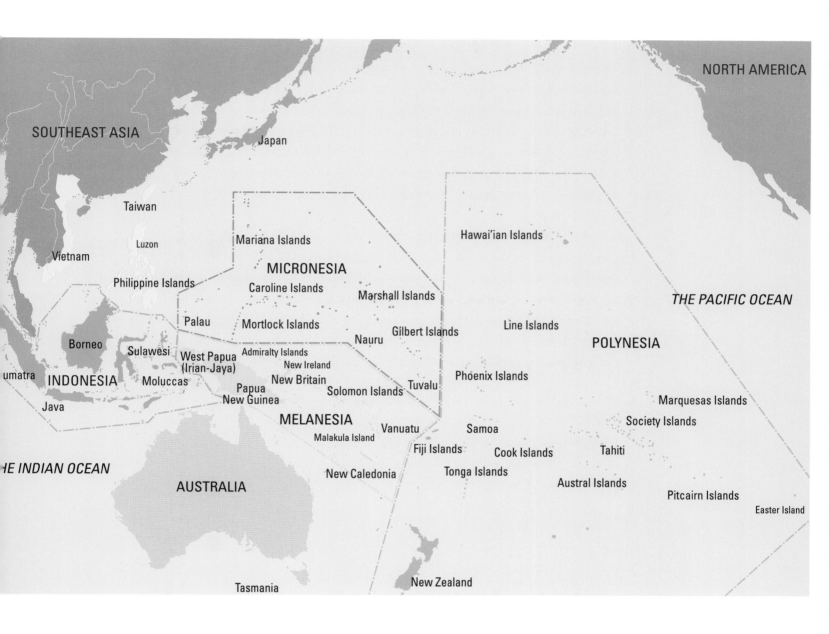

NORTH AMERICA

SOUTHEAST ASIA

Japan

Taiwan

Luzon

Vietnam

Philippine Islands

Mariana Islands

Hawai'ian Islands

MICRONESIA

THE PACIFIC OCEAN

Caroline Islands

Marshall Islands

Palau

Mortlock Islands

Line Islands

POLYNESIA

Nauru

Gilbert Islands

Borneo

Sulawesi

West Papua
(Irian-Jaya)

Admiralty Islands

New Ireland

Phoenix Islands

umatra

INDONESIA

Moluccas

New Britain

Tuvalu

Marquesas Islands

Java

Papua
New Guinea

Solomon Islands

Society Islands

MELANESIA

Vanuatu

Samoa

Tahiti

Malakula Island

Fiji Islands

Cook Islands

HE INDIAN OCEAN

AUSTRALIA

New Caledonia

Tonga Islands

Austral Islands

Pitcairn Islands

Easter Island

Tasmania

New Zealand

The Southeast Asia and Oceania sections are organized here by traditional cultural areas, rather than their current
political affiliations. Thus politically Kalimantan in Borneo, and West Papua (Irian Jaya) – the western part of the island
of New Guinea – are provinces of Indonesia. The eastern part of New Guinea, Papua New Guinea, is an independent
state that includes the Northwestern Islands, the Admiralty Islands, New Britain, New Ireland, and the (northern)
Solomon Islands. Australia, Nauru, New Zealand, Vietnam, the Philippines, Fiji, (western and southern) Solomon Islands,
and Tuvalu are also independent states. Hawaii is one of the United States of America. Easter Island is a province of
Chile. The Marquesas Islands are part of French Polynesia, and New Caledonia is a French overseas territory.

Southeast Asia

The central area of Vietnam comprises a great mountain range interrupted by river valleys and covered with dense forest. Living on the lower plateaus and valley floors are several groups of people who are the ancient, indigenous inhabitants of the country. The Vietnamese, who were later immigrants, call them collectively Moi, meaning "savages." The derogatory word is undeserved, since they are settled rice growers living in large family longhouses, who maintain a democratic social structure. All groups recognize the existence of divinities who govern various aspects of life, and who must be placated to ensure the success of agriculture and the well-being of the dead.

The group called the Jorai pay particular reverence to the souls of the deceased. After the immediate funeral of a clan member, a second funeral is held some time later, attended by the entire clan, to speed the soul on its way to the land of the dead. The main impetus for Jorai sculpture is the building of tombs. They are fenced with a structure of horizontal bars slotted into vertical posts. The upper ends of the posts are carved with a variety of subjects, including birds (peacocks, for instance) and riders on elephants. The most important are squatting figures of human beings, representing the deceased and his attendants or slaves.

Gift of Faith-dorian and Martin Wright, New York, to American Friends of the Israel Museum, in memory of Abraham Janoff

Dournes, 1988

Post from a tomb
Vietnam: Jorai
Late 19th – early 20th century
Wood
Height 190 cm
354.85

The indigenous peoples of Borneo are collectively known as Dayaks ("inland people"), a term that applies to a considerable number of languages and non-Muslim cultures. Kalimantan, comprising most of the eastern and southern parts of the island, is home to the large Kenyah and Kayan groups, among others.

Most Dayaks lived on the rivers in communities that were concentrated into a single building on high piles: the longhouse. This consisted of a gallery that functioned in many ways – as reception hall, social and ritual space, and even as a kind of street – off of which were compartments for family quarters. While most were smaller, some Kenyah longhouses reached a length of 350 meters and accommodated up to 600 people.

In front of each longhouse stood several posts carved with anthropomorphic images. (The term generally used, *hampatong*, applies to other figure carvings as well.) In this example, from the top of such a post, the figure is squatting with its hands clasped over its shins. What seems to be a miniature face protrudes from between its teeth. On the back of the figure's head is another, smaller face whose chin has been modified by subsequent recutting. The back of the figure bears a large, horned animal head.

These figures were set up to provide spiritual protection against evil supernaturals that might attempt to attack the members of the community; if approached by such spirits, they were said to emit warning cries.

Gift of Faith-dorian and Martin Wright, New York, to American Friends of the Israel Museum, in memory of Abraham Janoff

Seated figure (*hampatong*)
Borneo, East Kalimantan:
Kenyah-Kayan Dayaks
Late 19th – early 20th century
Wood
Height 65 cm
1159.78

The dominant figures in the Batak culture of central Sumatra were rulers and priest-magicians known as *datu*. The training of a *datu* was a long and costly process that involved education in literacy. The Batak comprised the only tribal group in Indonesia to develop a script, with characters based on Sanskrit, that was used mainly to record spells in concertina-style "books" made of bark. Besides books of spells, the *datu* owned equipment that included elaborately carved staffs and model weapons. The *datu* also mastered the secrets of the magic potions that constituted part of their equipment. Some were kept in small, antique Chinese pottery jars, highly valued throughout tribal Indonesia, while other containers were fashioned from buffalo horns. Both the jars and horns had elaborately carved wood stoppers.

The stoppers almost invariably include an image of the mythical animal *singa*, a combination of a horse, buffalo, elephant, and dragon. This rather mysterious beast may be related to a creator god who supports the world on his back. A constant theme of Batak art, the *singa* also figures in the architectural sculpture of their impressive houses and stone grave monuments. Here, the main *singa* head is flanked by two smaller *singa* with human riders, whose hands meet below the *singa*'s jaw. An additional human figure is placed below and in front of them.

Gift of Mr. and Mrs. Samuel Dubiner, Ramat Gan

Stopper for container of magic
materials (*nega morsarang*)
Indonesia, Sumatra: Toba Batak
Late 19th – early 20th century
Wood, paint
Height 23 cm
1066.2.56

The people of the southern Philippines are largely Muslims, and thus the art of the Sulu Archipelago has been strongly influenced by Islamic forms, particularly in its use of elaborate floral and abstract motifs, in a style called *ukkul*. At the same time, their art reveals significant traces of older Asian — and even Oceanic island — beliefs, manifested in the wooden grave monuments carved for important men and women. These monuments consist of a narrow horizontal element into which is set, at its middle, a vertical element. Both rest on a pair of crosspieces.

The treatment of the two parts indicates the sex of the deceased. Men's monuments have columnar uprights of somewhat phallic form; women's markers feature openwork panels topped with stylized representations of hair combs.

The horizontal parts, which are often rendered in *ukkul* style, are carved as images of horses, crocodiles, or the well-known mythical dragon of southeast Asia called *naga*. Sometimes they assume boatlike shapes, a resemblance enhanced by the crosspieces, which suggest outriggers. The overall form recalls the ancient concept, widespread in Indonesia and Oceania, of a "soul boat" or "ship of the dead" that ferried the deceased to the next world.

Gift of Faith-dorian and Martin Wright, New York, to American Friends of the Israel Museum, in memory of Abraham Janoff

Casino, 1981

Man's grave marker
Philippines, Sulu Archipelago:
probably Bajau people
Late 19th — early 20th century
Wood
Length 110 cm
B94.0416

The Ifugao live in the northern part of Luzon, itself the most northerly, and largest, of the Philippine Islands. The terrain is extremely mountainous and therefore not naturally suited to the cultivation of rice, the Ifugao's main crop, which requires flat, flooded fields. Like the people of Bali (among others), they have overcome this disadvantage by modeling the slopes, over many hundreds of years, into huge, spectacular terraces.

Fertility is one of the main concerns of the Ifugao religion, and though they have many gods presiding over various activities, including warfare, the most important are those governing the growth of rice. These deities have no individual names, but are referred to collectively as *bulul*, and they are represented by small wooden figures also known as *bulul.* The gods are shown in human form, male and female, standing or squatting on geometric pedestals in the form of rice containers. The making and consecration of these carvings by specialist sculptors is a long, expensive process. Once they are instated in the rice barns of their owners, they must be propitiated with frequent sacrifices of pigs' blood. *Bulul*, therefore, are solely the prerogative of people of wealth and high status who are able to afford the sacrifices.

Gift of Yvonne Belmont, New York, to American Friends of the Israel Museum

Ellis, 1981

Pair of figures (*bulul*)
Philippines, Luzon: Ifugao
Late 19th – early 20th century
Wood, sacrificial materials
Height 70, 71 cm
B92.819 (a–b)

The small island of Atauro, with a population of fewer than 5,000 people, lies among the lesser Sunda Islands, the most easterly group of Indonesia. The almost exclusive subject for their sculpture was their deified ancestors, represented by small figures, male and female, that were usually hung in clusters on trees. Their angular style is highly distinctive — and, in fact, unknown outside the island. Besides these small works, some rare, large sculptures were made in the form of poles with human heads. The figures represented two major deities, and were set up in pairs facing each other on stone cairns, or platforms, similar to those often built in other islands in eastern Indonesia.

Gift of Faith-dorian and Martin Wright, New York, to American Friends of the Israel Museum, in memory of Abraham Janoff

Duarte, 1990

Pair of figures
Indonesia, Atauro Island
19th century
Wood, fiber, cloth
Height 16, 17 cm
B91.222 (a–b)

In some islands of the southeastern Moluccas, a dais or platform of piled-up stones occupied the open central plazas of the villages, and was used as seating space during rituals and ceremonies. On these daises were erected tall wood carvings, towering well above the people, that served as village altars. They were made in several parts: a plain central post, rectangular in cross-section, with several other elements tenoned into its upper end, forming an elaborate composition. Posts of the same type seem also to have been set up in houses, as perhaps in this case.

Partway below the top of its angled upper part, the post is cut back to create a small niche, which holds the figure of a male ancestor – probably the founder of the village. In the typical pose of figures from these islands, he squats on a square plinth with his arms folded and resting on his drawn-up knees, leaning up against the post itself. The face, characteristically, consists of a flat plane under a rounded cranium, dominated by a huge blade of a nose. Otherwise nude, the figure is shown as wearing the ornaments of high-status men. Below, on either side, is a slightly crescent-shaped form; together, these represent the ends of a boat. In this case, their terminals are carved as roosters, often shown on boat prows as symbols of fertility, aggression, prowess, and – by extension – dominance and wealth. The heavy beam extending at right angles to the back of the post is another stylized representation of a boat, itself an object replete with cosmic symbolism in the islands of Indonesia, and indeed throughout the Pacific islands at large. From a stick tied underneath it dangle cowrie shells, additional symbols of the sea and wealth. In some of these altars, a short bar supporting a small offering-cup extends forward under the figure, but it is absent here.

Gift of the Faith-dorian and Martin Wright Family, New York, to American Friends of the Israel Museum

Taylor and Aragon, 1990

Altar post
Indonesia, Moluccas, Leti Island
Late 19th – early 20th century
Wood
Height 132 cm
B01.0041

Australia

The religious life of the Aborigines of Australia was largely based upon the myths describing the creation of the world by human and animal ancestors, and ritual often entailed the symbolic reenactment of scenes from such myths. Owing to the constraints of the environment, limitations on available materials, and the Aborigines' nomadic way of life, the staging of ritual was elaborate but ephemeral in its means. Any structures involved were slight, though large designs were painted or grooved into the ground. Costume consisted of body decoration, which included paint, large quantities of bird down stuck to the skin, and totemic emblems carried on the head. These two hats are examples of such emblems, which in some cases could be of great size.

Gifts of Mr. and Mrs. C. T. Shipman, Toorak, Australia

Two ceremonial hats
Australia, Northern Territory,
Mornington Island: Lardil
Late 19th – early 20th century
Human hair, emu feathers,
paint, bark
Height 60, 42 cm
1400.77, 1399.77

The spear-thrower is a weapon of enormous antiquity: the earliest examples known were made by the Magdalenians of Europe about 20,000 BCE. More recently, it was employed in Precolumbian America by the Maya, Aztecs, and others; by Native American groups; and in recent times by the Inuit. In the Pacific region it was used by the New Guinea people of the Sepik River in the northeast, and the Marind-Anim of the southwest. The Australian Aborigines seem to have invented it independently about 7,000 years ago.

At its simplest, the spear-thrower is no more than a length of cord attached to the butt end of a spear, but it has assumed many more permanent and elaborate forms. The most common ones are rods or oval plaques – always with a grip at one end and a peg at the other – against which the butt of the spear rests. Used with an overhand swing, it increases the length of the human arm, and thus improves the range and velocity of light spears by up to 100 meters.

The Aborigines used the plaque-type spear-thrower mainly in the western areas and the central desert of the continent, while the bar type was used in the north and east. The flat surfaces of the plaques offered fields for engraved designs, which naturally could not be found on the northern spear-throwers. However, it is typical of the Aborigines' economical instinct for style that they could transform even these simple items into objects of refined elegance.

In this example, the three elements complement one another both in color and form. The long, plain slat of dark wood contrasts in color and form with the white oval shell at one end, and in form, with the short, straight peg at the other. Austerely functional, the spear-thrower achieves an abstract beauty.

Gift of Mr. and Mrs. C. T. Shipman, Toorak, Australia

Spear-thrower
Australia, north Queensland, Cape York
Late 19th – early 20th century
Wood, shell, resin
Length 77 cm
1372.77

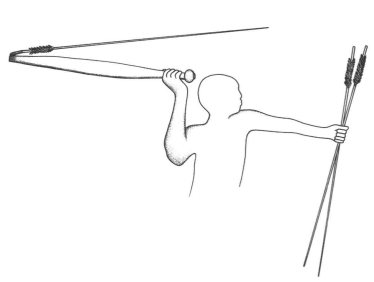

The islands off the north coast of Australia on which the Tiwi people live are relatively isolated, and perhaps for this reason their art has developed in an individual direction. Their painting style stresses bold bands of color framing large areas of cross-hatching and dots, unlike that of most of the other Australian Aboriginal groups, which relies heavily on line drawing.

The Tiwi's most spectacular works are tall carved posts erected in groups for a cycle of funerary ceremonies called Pukumani ("mourners"). The posts are cut so as to form a vertical series of cylinders of varying diameters, and are painted with apparently abstract but actually meaningful designs.

Pukumani includes the performance of specially composed songs, dancing through fires, and the presentation of valuable goods that are packed in bark bags such as this one and deposited on the tops of the poles. The bags, made by women and usually painted by men (but perhaps also by women), were also used in other ritual contexts. The meanings of their designs — if they had any — are obscure.

The Australian Aboriginal tradition of painting on flat surfaces such as rock, bark, or human skin, certainly dates back many millennia. Paint was being traded for quite long distances, if only for body decoration, some 30,000 years ago. The Aboriginal art of rock painting may go back 20,000 years — that is, to the time of the famous Paleolithic cave paintings of Europe — or even longer. Painting on bark, which is obviously a highly perishable type of support, may be as old or much more recent; no archaeological evidence exists to confirm either possibility.

The painting of a barramundi, a prized food fish, is rendered in the famous "X-ray" style of northern Australia. In this style, the subject to be shown — usually an animal, but sometimes a human — is outlined in silhouette. Within the outline, the internal organs are drawn in a stylized way. The exterior appearance and the interior reality are thus shown simultaneously, to convey to the viewer the totality of the creature.

Painting: Gift of Mary Wolfers, Sydney, in honor of the Silver Jubilee of WIZO Nahalal of Sydney, by the president and committee, 1962

Bag: Gift of Mr. and Mrs. C. T. Shipman, Toorak, Australia

Painting of a barramundi fish
Australia, probably western Arnhem
Land, Oenpelli
Late 19th – early 20th century
Bark, paint
Length 60 cm
3449.12.63

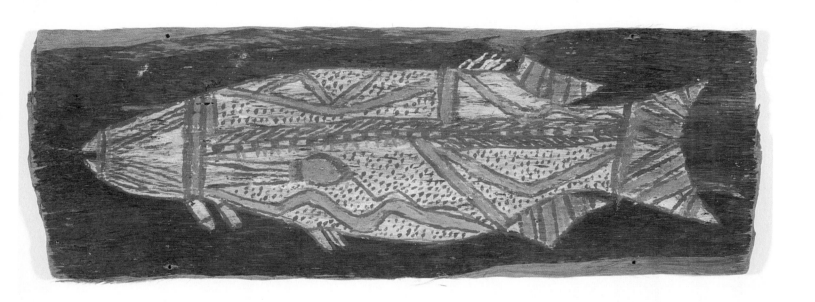

Bag
Australia, Northern Territory,
Bathurst and Melville Islands: Tiwi
Late 19th — early 20th century
Stringy-bark tree bark, paint
Height 33 cm
83.07.89

This shield is the typical flat, leaf-shaped model of the south Australian area; its decoration is also typical. The front side is divided in half by a narrow, vertical engraved line that widens at the middle of the field. Here there are two large perforations for attaching a flexible strip of wood, used as a handle, which is now missing.

The rest of the surface, but for a narrow tab at each end, is filled with tightly spaced horizontal rows of chevrons, engraved with an animal's tooth; these are also subtly divided laterally, by changes of pattern, into upper and lower areas. It is likely that the lines were originally filled with white clay, producing a dazzling effect.

Formerly in the Sir Henry Wellcome Collection
Gift of Douglas Newton, New York, to American Friends of the Israel Museum

Broad shield
Australia, South Australia,
Murray River area
Probably 19th century
Wood
Height 82 cm
B99.1337

New Guinea

In the Pacific islands, where the wheel was never invented, and where there were no beasts of burden in any case, only two means of travel existed. People moved about by foot on land, and by canoe and boat on the rivers and seas. The vessels existed in a number of forms and sizes, from small canoes paddled by a single passenger to big seagoing boats equipped with matting sails and crewed by up to several dozen men. The basic part of the vessel was always a hull carved from a single tree trunk — sometimes doubled, in the case of large vessels — with built-up sides and outriggers for added stability.

The main use of all these watercraft was the pursuit of trade and warfare. At the same time, they were closely associated with the supernatural world of the ancestors whom, in some cases, they actually represented. In other instances they were built as symbolic models of the cosmos as their makers conceived it.

Every important vessel was richly decorated with carved and painted ornamentation, particularly at the prow but often at the stern as well. (Indeed, many canoes were designed to be sailed either end first.) The most frequent form of these terminal decorations, on the northern New Guinea coasts and the other Pacific islands in general, is a thin, upcurved wood panel, decorated in a variety of styles. At the Geelvink Bay of the western end of New Guinea, these panels are carved in openwork with complex scroll patterns, into which small depictions of the heads of ancestors are incorporated. The prows of large war canoes, used on slave-raiding expeditions, often sported several such panels as the emblems of different clans.

The small canoe prows of the islands east of Geelvink Bay are carved in the same general vertical/horizontal conformation. Here, however, instead of a flat panel we find a bird's head surmounted by a human figure. The designs on the side panels represent fish.

Wandamen canoe prow: Collected by Edward Klejman
Wandamen and Sobei canoe prows: Gifts of Faith-dorian and Martin Wright, New York, to American Friends of the Israel Museum, in memory of Abraham and Molly Janoff

Van Baaren, 1992; *Kooijman and Hoogebrugge*, 1992

Canoe prows
West Papua, Yamna-Wakde coast:
Sobei
Late 19th – early 20th century
Wood
Length 55.8, 57.1 cm
B95.0512 (a–b)

Canoe prow
West Papua, Geelvink Bay,
Wandamen Bay: Wandamen
Late 19th – early 20th century
Wood, cassowary feathers
Length 130 cm
556.82

The Asmat of West Papua live in the alluvial swampland plains that extend along much of New Guinea's southwestern coast. Until recently, their villages were in constant conflict with one another: the Asmat were headhunters (and also cannibals), for whom the taking of enemy heads – and the acquisition of power concentrated in those heads – was the key to the attainment of strength and fertility. The passage from boyhood to manhood could only be effected by the taking of a head and the assumption of the victim's name. Death, then, came about through direct, violent murder – but also via the more subtle agency of enemy sorcery. In either case, the spirits of the dead demanded revenge. Thus, the Asmat became locked into a tragic, self-perpetuating cycle of killing.

The preparations for head-hunting included a ritual to commemorate those to be avenged. A tree, or several trees, were felled and brought to the village – a highly symbolic action, as human beings were believed to have been created from carved wooden figures. The trunks were then carved into the poles called *mbish*, in the general form of the mythological spirit-canoes that carried souls to the afterworld. The enormously exaggerated "prows" displayed figures of the dead and large, phallic openwork panels. The *mbish* were set up in the village and celebrated with drumming, songs, and dances. After the ensuing head-hunting raid, they were carried back to the jungle and abandoned to decay in the swamps where sago palms grew. (Sago is the major source of food in lowlands New Guinea.) The poles were supposed to promote the palms' fertility.

On the *mbish* depicted here, the upper figure carries a child on his back. The panel features hornbill heads and the tails of opossums, symbols of head-hunting. The head held by the lower figure probably illustrates the custom of having a boy undergoing initiation sit with a newly taken head between his legs. (The canoe-shaped lower section is not shown.)

Collected by Pierre-Dominique Gaisseau, 1959
Gift of Faith-dorian and Martin Wright, New York, to American Friends of the Israel Museum, in memory of Abraham Janoff

Smidt, 1993

Section of a ritual pole (*mbish*)
West Papua, Casuarinen Coast: Asmat
Late 19th – early 20th century
Wood, paint
Height 530 cm
B87.131

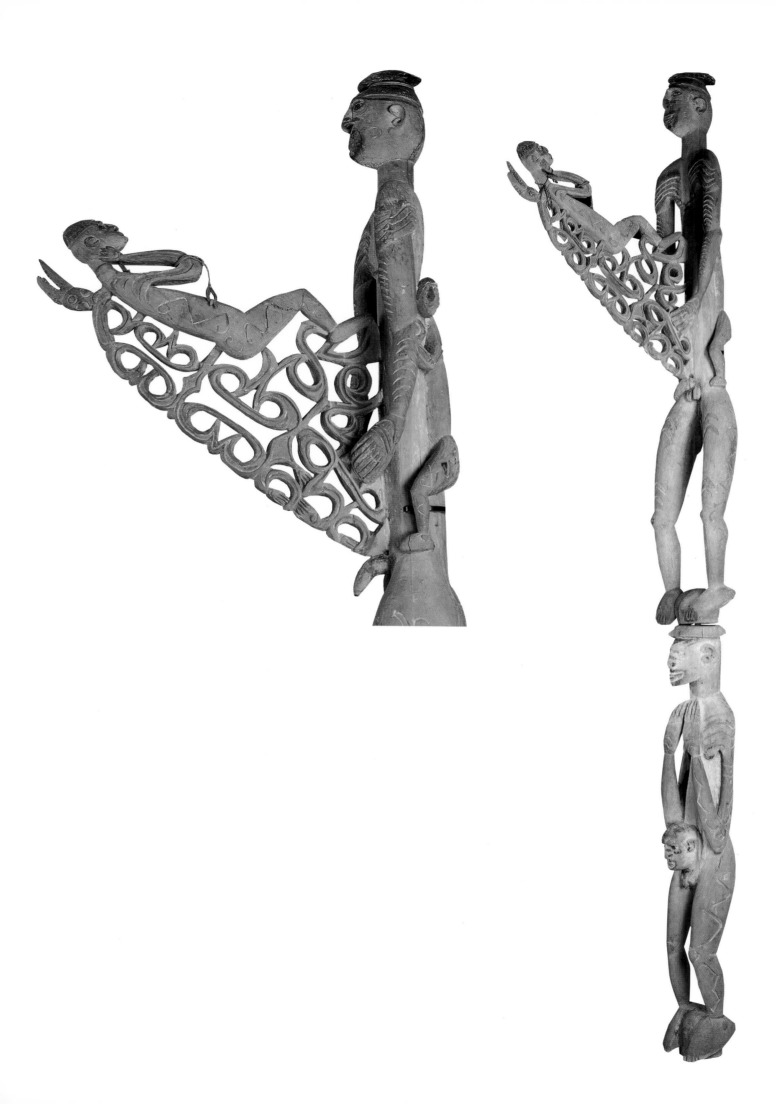

Wooden bowls and platters for serving food were used everywhere in the Pacific islands, and almost everywhere bore carved decoration on their undersides, as in these two examples.

The Lake Sentani platters are usually oval and very shallow. Sometimes (as here), the carving included a pierced handle for suspension. The low relief design in this example shows a frog.

The small Tami Islands in the Huon Gulf of northeast New Guinea have few natural advantages and, thus, trade was essential to the people's economic life. The most famous products of these people were their carved wooden bowls, highly valued and much sought after by neighboring groups of islanders. The bowls are usually elliptical and deep-bodied, elegantly carved in shallow relief at one or both ends with human heads wearing three-pointed headdresses, and with stylized shell ornaments, fish, turtles, birds, and other designs on the sides.

It is said that, originally, the designs were often the copyright of individual carvers — but these rights have been infringed in recent years. Owing to the inability of the Tami Island carvers to keep up with the demand for their bowls, workers on neighboring islands, and even on New Britain to the north, began making identical copies. The Tami style has thus become distributed over a wide area.

Bowl: Formerly in the collection of Jay C. Leff
Platter and bowl: Gifts of Faith-dorian and Martin Wright, New York, to American Friends of the Israel Museum, in memory of Abraham Janoff

Kooijman, 1959; Bodrogi, 1961

Platter
West Papua, Lake Sentani: Sentani
Late 19th – early 20th century
Wood
Length 42 cm
B77.0314

Bowl
Papua New Guinea, Morobe Province,
Huon Gulf: Tami
Late 19th – early 20th century
Wood
Length 106 cm
B82.0553

There are approximately sixty to seventy pottery industries in Papua New Guinea, most located along the northern coast and its hinterland. The main products are vessels for the storage, cooking, and serving of food but, in the past, ceramic vessels have also been used for secondary burials of human bones. In nearly all cases, pottery-making is a cooperative craft in which women or men make the basic pots (usually by the coiling method), men decorate them, and women perform the final firing. While each industry tends to be concentrated in a particular village or group of villages, many engage in thriving export systems that distribute their products over wide areas.

Among the Adzera people, pottery is semi-sacred work performed by men, who keep some of its processes secret. Pots are decorated with incised patterns and molded figures. In this example, the small creatures at the rim are flying foxes. Formerly, pots were items used in marriage payments, though this practice is now obsolete. Nevertheless, unlike many other New Guinea pottery industries, the Adzera's has remained active in recent years and, to a certain extent, the trade in their wares has even expanded.

The pottery style of the Kombio people in the foothills of the Torricelli Mountains has been copied by several neighboring groups. Only two types of vessels are made — both by men; these are cooking pots and food-serving bowls. The bowls are decorated with a narrow range of designs formed by applying thin clay strips to their surfaces. The motifs are representations of leaves (the circles) and uncoiling ferns (the spiral with a "tail") (see also p. 265).

Gifts of Mr. and Mrs. C. T. Shipman, Toorak, Australia

May and Tuckson, 1982

Vessel
Papua New Guinea,
Morobe Province: Adzera
Late 19th – early 20th century
Clay
Height 12 cm
76.73.88

Vessel
Papua New Guinea, East Sepik Province,
Torricelli Mountains: Kombio
Late 19th – early 20th century
Clay
Height 18.5 cm
70.89.291

The Sepik River, one of the longest in New Guinea, flows from west to east across the two large provinces (West Sepik and East Sepik) named after it. At its effluent in the east, it is flanked to the west by a number of lagoons surrounding small islands. On the seashore and the islands stand the villages of the Murik people.

Masters of the craft of building large sailing ships, the Murik have come to dominate a trading complex in their special manufactures for many kilometers along the coast. They supply a diverse range of commodities – from food and such wares as baskets, to ritual cycles with their associated songs and masks. Consequently, they have not only achieved prosperity, but have also exercised a profound influence on the cultures and art styles of their clients.

Unlike most Sepik communities, the Murik had an actual pantheon of deified ancestors who were the objects of regular cults: male ancestors for men, female for women – an unusual occurrence in an area where generally only men participated in religion. These deities were believed to inhabit their large wood images (metaphorically called their "canoes") when invoked by ritual experts.

The crisp, sharply defined style of this mask is typical of Murik art, as is the enormously elongated nose. Large masks represented the god-ancestors, and were displayed on racks in the ceremonial houses when they were not being employed in dances.

Gift of Mr. and Mrs. C. T. Shipman, Toorak, Australia, and Maureen and Harold Zarember, New York, to American Friends of the Israel Museum

Mask (*brag*)
Papua New Guinea, East Sepik
Province coast, Murik Lakes:
Murik
Late 19th – early 20th century
Wood, paint
Height 32 cm
B96.0601

Small standing figures of males and females were carved in large numbers in the northeast coastal areas of Papua New Guinea. Some of them were traded westward for very long distances by the Murik living near the mouth of the Sepik River. Their significance is not well known, but it is likely that they functioned in magic, as amulets, and as figures of ancestors, commemorated the recently dead, or served all these purposes at once.

The lavish adornment of this figure demonstrates that it was highly esteemed. A small crocodile carved on each leg indicates a connection with mythology, as does the face, which replicates a *brag* (mask). The head suggests the headdress formerly worn by Murik men, in which the hair was pulled through a long, upright basketry tube.

Formerly in the Museum für Völkerkunde, Dresden, no. 21458
Gift of Dr. Alfred and Cynthia Hess, New York, to American Friends of the Israel Museum, in memory of Hyman Rabinowitz

Male figure
Papua New Guinea, East Sepik Province
coast, Murik Lakes: Murik
Late 19th – early 20th century
Wood, paint, fiber, shells,
flying-fox teeth
Height 83 cm
B95.0523

This elegant ghost of a formerly more elaborate carving still retains all its essential original characteristics. It is a representative of the so-called hook style that is prevalent south of the Sepik River, as well as among the Abelam between the river and the northern coast (see p. 255).

The Alamblak, a population now much diminished by epidemics, lived in hilltop villages above the Karawari River, a southern Sepik tributary. Their *yipwon* carvings are characterized by a narrow, vertical spine curving into a hook at the upper end. Below this is a human head, then a series of hooks in concentric groups. A short leg (missing here) forms the lower end. The hooks represent the ribs and heart of a skeletal being.

Yipwon were made in large versions, up to three meters high, which constituted images of the patron spirits of clans. Tiny examples were made as men's personal amulets. The spirits primarily governed good fortune and success in war and hunting; for their assistance, they received rubbed-on offerings of the blood and excrement of the kill.

Sometimes, on the deaths of their owners, *yipwon* were deposited with the corpses in the rock shelters of the mountains; it is this treatment that accounts for the worn condition of many of them.

Collected by Nils Madsen, about 1965
Gift of Douglas Newton, New York, and the Faith-dorian and Martin Wright Family, New York, to American Friends of the Israel Museum

Haberland and Seyfarth, 1974; *Haberland*, 1968

Figure (*yipwon*)
Papua New Guinea, East Sepik
Province, Karawari River: Alamblak
16th–18th century
Wood
Height 149 cm
B98.1062

The Ewa formerly lived south of the Alamblak but, owing to the effects of similar epidemics, became reduced to about 120 people who now live dispersed among other groups. Their basic style resembled the Alamblak's in general, but with different motifs of elaborate design on the basic spines instead of simple hooks. Nevertheless, their figures served the same functions as the *yipwon*. Like the *yipwon*, many have been found in rock shelters. Several have been dated as about 300 to 600 years old.

Small wooden heads of this type were the most sacred objects of the Ewa. Their name, *koa ngginggi*, means "house Mother," for they represented the mythical mother of the men's ceremonial houses. When a new house was inaugurated, a figure of the Mother was built of plants, and the carving was fitted to it as a head. As a rule, they consist only of the head and a rodlike neck; the hook below the chin of this one is unusual.

The Bahinemo, currently numbering about 300 people, are another group living in the mountains west of the Alamblak and Ewa. Their small villages, consisting of no more than a few dwellings and a ceremonial house, are often deserted during the long expeditions the Bahinemo make to the forests for hunting and food-gathering. Initiations and other ritual occasions are the main times that the people assemble in the villages as a community.

The sacred objects, collectively called *gara* but also having personal names, are slit-gongs with carved finials, decorated flutes, and two types of carvings in the hook style. One of the types is an elliptical panel with a vertical row of concentric hooks centering on a ring or disk with annular eyes on each side of it, and a mouth at the foot of the panel. The other is a spine with only the hooks and disk, as in this example. It is not clear what these carvings represent. Several explanations exist — and are presumably all correct, depending on the speaker's point of view. The central disk is probably a symbol of the sun or moon, as in other carvings; the hooks may be hornbill beaks. The whole image may be a catfish, in accordance with the fact that all the carvings are associated with water-spirits.

The Arthur and Madeleine Chalette Lejwa Collection, bequeathed by Madeleine Chalette Lejwa to American Friends of the Israel Museum

Dye, in *Lutkehaus et al.*, 1980; *Newton*, 1971

Cult figure (*gara*)
Papua New Guinea, East Sepik
Province, Hunstein Mountains:
Bahinemo
Late 19th – early 20th century
Wood, paint
Height 89.5 cm
B00.1697

Figure (*koa ngginggi*)
Papua New Guinea,
East Sepik Province,
Karawari River area: Ewa
Late 19th – early 20th century
Wood, paint
Height 60 cm
B00.0679

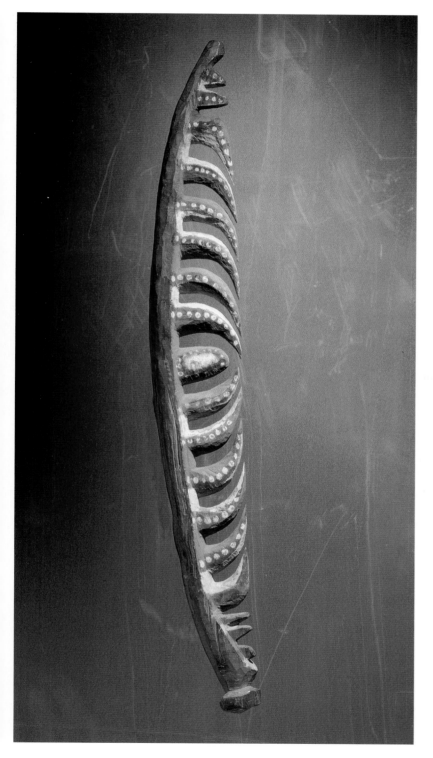
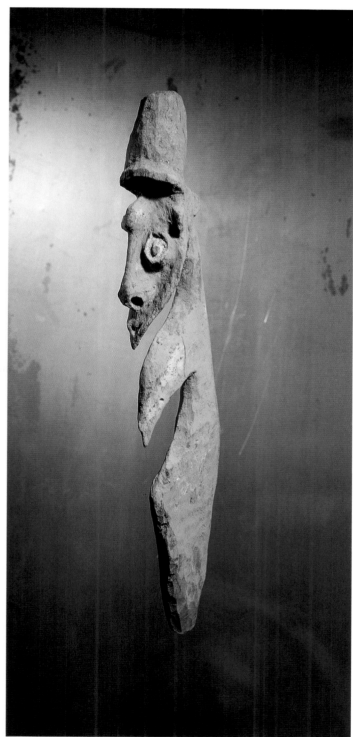

The Abelam, numbering some 40,000 people, are the largest single group in the Sepik provinces. Their steeply hilly environment is ideal for the growth of yams, their main crop, upon which one of their principal cults is based. Prolific artists and ambitious architects, they build enormous triangular ceremonial houses with gables rising to twenty meters or more.

Although their name means "grandfather," *nggwalndu* are neither ancestors nor culture heroes, but male spirits associated with water holes and swamps. Involved in an initiatory cult of their own, they are embodied in huge faces painted on ceremonial-house gables and in large carved figures that are among the most secret of Abelam sacred objects. Usually the figures are anthropomorphic and quite naturalistic. Some, however, like the *yipwon* of the Alamblak, show human heads at the top of registers of opposed hooks. This style is said to have preceded the naturalistic one.

On this figure, the head is crowned with a crest that replicates the small woven or carved ornaments worn by men during ritual, and that also appears worn by the painted *nggwalndu* faces. The "hooks" are stylized birds' heads, probably totemic, and seemingly of hornbills.

Gift of Mr. and Mrs. Cedric H. Marks, New York, to American Friends of the Israel Museum

Forge, 1965, 1973; *Hauser-Schaublin,* 1989

Figure (*nggwalndu*)
Papua New Guinea, East Sepik
Province, Prince Alexander Mountains:
Abelam
Late 19th – early 20th century
Wood, paint
Height 168 cm
265.80

North of the upper Sepik River lies a small range of hills inhabited by the Kwoma people; the Nukuma people live in the swamplands beyond. These two groups speak dialects of the same language and largely share a common culture. In particular, their mythologies and cults are identical. Their art styles, however, are somewhat different.

The major cult centers on the planting, cultivation, and harvesting of yams. While not their chief food (as with most Sepik cultures, the nutritional staple is the flour produced from the sago palm), yams have great symbolic significance, and relate to male power and fertility. The most important rituals take place in a cycle of three ceremonies at the time when the yams are harvested. Each ritual has associated carvings that are then displayed in the ceremonial house. As usual, the carvings are not to be seen by women, though the women are expected at certain times to participate in the singing, which goes on almost uninterruptedly during a day and a night for each performance.

Yena is the first ritual in the cycle, and shares its name with the wooden heads made for it. Although there are several explanations for them, the heads generally seem to represent clan spirits.

Kwoma head (B95.0513): Collected 1973
Smaller Nukuma head (B99.0881): Collected 1965; *Bowden*, 1983
Gifts of Douglas Newton, New York, to American Friends of the Israel Museum

Larger Nukuma head (77.44.61): Gift of Mr. and Mrs. C. T. Shipman, Toorak, Australia

Head (*yena*)
Papua New Guinea, East Sepik
Province, Tongwindjamb: Kwoma
Carved ca. 1945
Wood, paint
Height 171.5 cm
B95.0513

Head (*yena*)
Papua New Guinea, East Sepik
Province: Nukuma
Late 19th – early 20th century
Wood, paint, feathers
Height 93 cm
77.44.61

Head (*yena*)
Papua New Guinea, East Sepik
Province, Amaki: Nukuma
Late 19th – early 20th century
Wood, paint (partial restoration
on the right cheek)
Height 44.5 cm
B99.0881

Many groups in the Sepik River area of Papua New Guinea make paintings on sago palm bark – or, botanically speaking, the broad, tough petioles that support the leaf. The petioles are cut, flattened, and sometimes linked in pairs to provide a wider surface. Usually the subjects relate to beings, and thus to incidents, in mythology.

Kambot paintings seem to have been used as screens dividing the most sacred part of the ceremonial house from the rest. Recent research suggests that some paintings showing several figures have a narrative element relating to mythological events. In this example, the single motif represents a stage in the gestation of a human female embryo.

The Iwam painting is by an important man named Nauni, who built a communal house, in the traditional conical style, at Burumai village on the May River, an upper Sepik tributary. The paintings in this house ran horizontally around the low walls between the roof and the floor. (The house was abandoned on his death some years before 1964.) Individual Iwam designs are often given more than one interpretation, but the central circle of this example is said to be a hair ornament.

The Kwoma painting shows repetitions of a motif – which recurs frequently in their art – consisting of a central oval element with curving forms on either side. These represent flying foxes (abu gimbi) or, rather, women transformed into the animals, which figure prominently in an incident of the Kwoma myth about the origin of humanity. Such paintings were attached to the ceilings of ceremonial houses.

Kambot painting: Gift of Ayala Zacks Abramov, Jerusalem

Iwam and Kwoma paintings: Collected 1965
Gifts of Douglas Newton, New York, to American Friends of the Israel Museum

Painting
Papua New Guinea, East Sepik
Province, Keram River: Kambot
Late 19th – early 20th century
Sago bark, paint
Height 94 cm
75.43.178

Painting
Papua New Guinea, East Sepik
Province, May River, Burumai: Iwam
Late 19th – early 20th century
Sago bark, paint
Height 111 cm
B95.0514

Painting
Papua New Guinea, East Sepik
Province, Beglam: Seserman Kwoma
Late 19th – early 20th century
Sago bark, paint
Height 126 cm
B95.0516

Armed conflict, in various degrees of intensity, was endemic in Pacific island life, and in many if not all areas, the successful warrior was highly regarded; the unsuccessful, conversely, was despised. This was especially true in New Guinea, where, generally speaking, a highly competitive and individualistic ethos prevailed among men.

The offensive weapons of New Guinea were mainly the spear and the bow and arrow which, in different forms, and to different extents (according to locality), could be used either for fighting or hunting. Defense was provided most often by the shield, though it was not employed universally. Some shields were made of pig or crocodile hide stretched on a cane frame, but the majority consisted of carved wood panels. Styles and dimensions ranged from great planks that could shelter several men to small plaques hung on the back. The usual forms were rectangular or oval, with vividly painted relief or incised designs on their outer surfaces. These designs are nearly always representations of spirits, intended to terrify the enemy, and are often heraldic, being clan emblems as well.

Both of these shields come from a range of mountains, the Torricellis, running parallel to the coast of northeast New Guinea. One, of uncertain provenance, is in a typical rectangular form; it features decorative bands at head and foot, with a central panel divided by cross-lines into quadrants containing circles at the crossing and at the widest points above and below. The design resembles some of those found on Kombio pottery (see p. 245); it is possible that the shield was from their area.

The Olo shield has parallel curved edges – a form not used by any other New Guinea people. The relief on the front of Olo shields is always the same basic cruciform design, with minor variations. Its exact meaning is unknown; in fact, a researcher was recently told – long after the use of shields became obsolete – that it is merely decorative. Nevertheless, it was probably linked, in the past, to the representative of a spirit – as was the rule elsewhere.

Gifts of Mr. and Mrs. C. T. Shipman, Toorak, Australia

Shield
Papua New Guinea, East Sepik
Province, Torricelli Mountains: Olo
Late 19th – early 20th century
Wood
Height 90 cm
70.4.82

Shield
Papua New Guinea, East Sepik
Province, Torricelli Mountains:
undetermined group
Late 19th – early 20th century
Wood
Height 182 cm
72.44.91

The Gulf of Papua is a vast body of water occupying about half the south coast of Papua New Guinea. All around it, and for many miles inland, are stretches of swampland cut through by many large, winding rivers and small creeks. Their deltas are interspersed with a multitude of small, low islands. A number of different groups of people inhabit this area. Several were fervent headhunters and cannibals; all were prolific and accomplished artists.

The headhunters' trophies were stripped of flesh and were usually kept in the men's ceremonial houses; sometimes they had features modeled over the skull or were otherwise decorated. For some festivals they were mounted on staffs and carried by their possessors or set up on the banks of rivers. Wooden carvings of heads or skulls on short shafts were used for the same purpose.

Collected by Thomas Schultze-Westrum, 1966
Gift of Evelyn A. J. Hall, Palm Beach, Florida, to American Friends of the Israel Museum

Head on shaft
Papua New Guinea, Gulf Province,
Goaribari Island: Kerewa (Kerebo)
Late 19th – early 20th century
Wood
Height 40 cm
162.84

Most of the people of the Gulf of Papua made great oval masks that could reach up to four meters in height, but were of very light construction. Cane frames were covered with sheets of bark-cloth to which thin cane strips were sewn, outlining designs. These were then filled in with color — generally black, white, red, and brown. The masks had round eyes and, in some cases, long freestanding noses and jaws. In the eastern part of the Gulf, among the Elema people, the masks were used in a cult of sea spirits, but this was not necessarily the case to the west. Unfortunately, little is known of their function in that area, but it seems that they might have appeared at boys' initiations.

This example, of completely traditional form, incorporates not only traditional materials but also, with typical ingenuity, one that is entirely Western — canvas. This sturdy import was available to the people any time between the beginning of European influence in the late nineteenth century and the breakdown of the native cultures by about 1940. It was, however, rarely used for such a work.

The long, oval form recurs throughout the art of the Gulf people. Besides in masks, it was also used for large, flat wooden boards that were carved with relief images. It is also the shape of bullroarers, the carved wooden slats whirled on the end of a cord that produce an uncanny booming noise, impersonating supernatural voices. It seems that these three types of objects were, in a sense, symbolic of one another and were ranked in grades of ascending sanctity, the bullroarers being the most sacred — and secret — of all.

Gift of Faith-dorian and Martin Wright, New York, to American Friends of the Israel Museum, in memory of Abraham Janoff

Mask (*keweke*)
Papua New Guinea, Gulf Province,
Era River–Wapo Creek area
Late 19th – early 20th century
Cane, wood, bark-cloth, canvas,
paint, fiber
Height 213 cm
350.85

While all art styles of the Gulf of Papua shared an emphasis on two-dimensional design, each had strongly individual qualities. This is well exemplified in the carved oval boards (*gope, kwoi, hohao,* and other local names) that were made in large numbers by all of them and kept in the men's houses. They are by far the most prevalent of Gulf works; many hundreds were made and still exist. Three-dimensional figure sculpture is, by comparison, rare. The low-relief designs on the boards are apparently images of protective spirits.

The four examples shown here come from the people living around the Gulf coast from west to east, and illustrate some of the variations to be found on a single theme. The Turamarubi (western Gulf) and Kerewa (central Gulf) *gope*s each depict within the confines of the slab a complete single figure in a semi-naturalistic manner. The *gope* from the inland Era River, on the other hand, features a separate head and a system of relief bands and abstracted limbs around a central navel. In the Purari River (eastern Gulf) *kwoi*, the main feature is simply the face.

Turamarubi board: Gift of Mr. and Mrs. Cedric H. Marks, New York, to American Friends of the Israel Museum

Kerewa board: Gift of Faith-dorian and Martin Wright, New York, to American Friends of the Israel Museum, in memory of Abraham Janoff

Era River and Purari River boards: Gifts of Mr. and Mrs. Cedric H. Marks, New York, to the America-Israel Cultural Foundation

Newton, 1961

Board (*gope*)
Papua New Guinea, Gulf Province,
Turama River: Turamarubi
Late 19th – early 20th century
Wood, paint
Height 138 cm
269.80

Board (*gope*)
Papua New Guinea, Gulf Province,
Goaribari Island: Kerewa (Kerebo)
Late 19th – early 20th century
Wood, paint
Height 123 cm
317.77

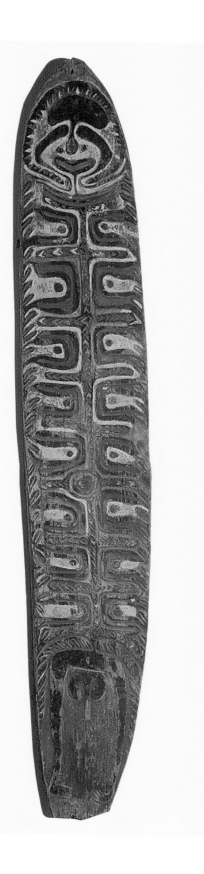

Board (*gope*)
Papua New Guinea,
Gulf Province,
Era River, Tetihui village
Late 19th – early 20th century
Wood, paint
Height 88 cm
106.4.65

Board (*kwoi*)
Papua New Guinea, Gulf Province,
Purari River: Purari
Late 19th – early 20th century
Wood, paint
Height 112 cm
107.4.65

As well as *gope* boards, the people of the Era River carved silhouetted human figures, often with two pairs of arms: one raised, one lowered. These were placed standing on or over the skulls of pigs and crocodiles that were laid in rows on the ceremonial house floor. Human trophy skulls were set in racks above them.

Gift of Evelyn A. J. Hall, Palm Beach, Florida, to American Friends of the Israel Museum

Figure (*bioma*)
Papua New Guinea, Gulf Province,
Era River
Late 19th – early 20th century
Wood, paint
Height 81 cm
160.84

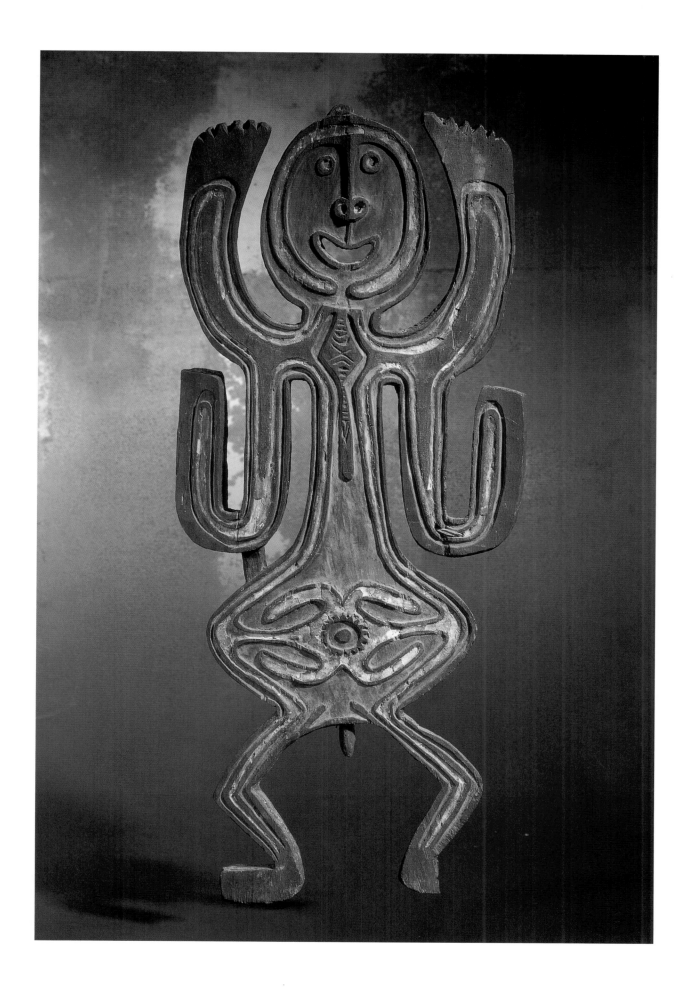

Widely scattered around the far southeastern tip of New Guinea are a number of islands which, together, constitute what is conventionally known as the Massim area. The islands are united by the Kula, the best known of the many New Guinea trade systems. Although many other goods are involved, the basis of the network is the circulation among trading partners of prestigious shell ornaments: necklaces, which pass in a clockwise direction through the circuit of islands, and armlets, which move counterclockwise. This institution is one of the few traditional aspects of New Guinea culture that have remained vital until recent years.

The vehicles of trade are large sailing canoes (*masawa* or *nagega*), which are built symmetrically so that they can be steered with either end forward. Great investments of time and labor are expended on these impressive vessels, which include extensive carved ornamentation (the most important being prow carvings), thin boards slotted into the prows on the line of the vessels, and lateral washboards just behind them that keep spray out of the canoe. The content of the carvings is a rich complex of protective symbols.

There are two major styles of canoe prow carvings and washboards. The first, roughly speaking, is used throughout the western part of the area that includes the Trobriand Islands and the d'Entrecastaux Islands. This style is represented here by the washboard (*lagimu*).

The other style, employed throughout nearly all the other islands and archipelagoes, is exemplified by the prow carving (*tabuya*), which approximates an asymmetrical crescent, with the upright lobe larger than the other. In this area, a small carving (*munkuris*) representing totemic birds is attached to the flange at the top of the prow board.

Canoe prow carving: Gift of Mr. and Mrs. C. T. Shipman, Toorak, Australia

Canoe washboard: Promised gift of Arthur Abrams, New Guinea

Beran and Meyer, 1987; *Newton*, 1975; *Scoditti*, 1990

Canoe prow carving (*tabuya*)
Papua New Guinea, Milne Bay
Province, southern area
Late 19th – early 20th century
Wood
Length 150 cm
72.44.52

Canoe washboard (*lagimu*)
Papua New Guinea, Milne Bay
Province, Trobriand Islands or
d'Entrecastaux Islands
Late 19th – early 20th century
Wood
Height 55 cm
L-80.18

In the small islands of the Torres Strait, between New Guinea and Australia, a major medium for sculpture was turtle shell. The material has probably never been used anywhere else to the same extent, but it was certainly a longstanding tradition here. As early as 1606, the Spanish explorers Torres and de Prado noticed turtle-shell masks and figures during a visit to one of the islands. As with nineteenth-century works, these must have been composed of plates of turtle shell linked together with fiber ties.

Recent periods saw the creation of large figures of crocodiles for initiation ceremonies; none of these has survived. Smaller works took the form of masks that were complex combinations of images of fish, bird, and human features. Simpler masks represented the human face alone, embellished with human-hair wigs and beards. These seem to have been used in funerary ceremonies miming the transition of the deceased's spirit into the next world.

Gift of the Lipschitz Art Collections, New York, to American Friends of the Israel Museum

Mask
Papua New Guinea, eastern Torres
Strait, Erub Island?: Meriam Mir
19th century
Turtle shell, fiber
Height 31 cm
B84.0148

Melanesia

The Admiralty Island group, lying to the northeast of New Guinea, includes the large island of Manus and a number of small islands to the east and south of it. The lack of many natural resources on some of the lesser islands has historically been offset by an abundance of certain specialized materials. The black volcanic glass, obsidian, widely use for tools and weapons, is one; it has been mined on the small islands for at least 4,500 years. Some islands developed specialized crafts, such as wood carving, and other forms of manufacture. The result was the creation of a network of trading throughout the archipelago, and the export of certain goods to destinations as far away as New Guinea and New Ireland.

Among the lesser works was a type of neck ornament worn by men who had achieved the prestigious status of homicide in warfare. Like some decorated bags used as homicidal regalia in New Guinea, the ornaments were worn on the back of the neck.

These examples are bundles of long, black frigate-bird feathers, notched and trimmed, attached to small carved heads or figures or, alternatively, to the upper bone of an ancestor. Hung at the nape, they stretched upwards at an angle to the man's body.

Neck ornament with head: Formerly in the H. Ian Hogbin Collection
Gift of Douglas Newton, New York, to American Friends of the Israel Museum, in memory of H. Ian Hogbin

Neck ornament with figure: Gift of Faith-dorian and Martin Wright, New York, to American Friends of the Israel Museum, in memory of Abraham Janoff

Ohnemus, 1996

Neck ornament with head (*keindin*)
Admiralty Islands
Late 19th – early 20th century
Wood, cut frigate-bird feathers
Length 49.5 cm
B98.0012

Neck ornament with figure (*kei*)
Admiralty Islands
Late 19th – early 20th century
Wood, paint, cut frigate-bird feathers
Length 42 cm
1167.78

The Baining are a people with several subgroups who live in the mountainous interior of northern New Britain. Their works of art consist almost entirely of figures, headpieces, and, above all, masks constructed of painted bark-cloth over cane frames. They differ from subgroup to subgroup, but the best-known masks are those called *kavat* made by the Kairak Baining.

A typical *kavat* has a protruding snout with gaping mouth and lolling tongue, above which is a flat panel (often bifurcated) on which are painted two large, owlish eyes. The masks are mainly left in the natural pale tint of the bark-cloth, but are sometimes also painted with fine geometrical patterns in red and black – the red being blood drawn from the makers' tongues. The effect is that of a grotesque, semi-human face; but, in fact, the Baining interpret the *kavat*s in a variety of ways. For them, the masks appear to represent a great number of the natural elements of their world. In recent times, the Baining have incorporated into *kavat* masks images of such markedly nontraditional elements as cattle and airplanes.

*Kavat*s appear at dances for deaths, marriages, and numerous other important occasions. The ceremonies take place at night around a large bonfire. The masqueraders wear only the masks and large bark-cloth phalli, their legs disguised with bunches of green leaves. They emerge one by one from the forest onto the dance ground, moving to the sound of singing and rhythms beaten on planks. When all are assembled, they dance together around and through the bonfire, often until dawn. The dancer's display of energy and endurance is a source of great prestige.

Gift of Mr. and Mrs. Arnold H. Maremont, Chicago, to American Friends of the Israel Museum

Corbin, 1979

Mask (*kavat*)
New Britain, Gazelle Peninsula:
Baining, Kairak subgroup
Late 19th – early 20th century
Bark-cloth, cane, paint
Height 94 cm
B76.0660

One of the two religious groups of the men of the Tolai, who live on the coast of northern New Britain, is a secret society called Inyet. Initiation into this organization is through the invitation of men's fathers and their mothers' brothers who are already members. Unlike the other society, Dukduk, which is largely involved with social controls, Inyet is mainly a cult of ancestors and indoctrination in the techniques of sorcery.

Among the objects used in the society are chalk carvings of animals and other creatures, which are said to serve a protective function. Every member of the society owns one such figure personally; the figures are supposed to maintain kinship relations with one another, which are reflected in the behavior of their owners.

Numerous wood carvings form part of the equipment of the Inyet ancestor cult, including openwork wands carried in dances and large figures of ancestors. Appropriately for an ancestor cult, among the cult's paraphernalia were mask-like objects made from the frontal skull bones of deceased society members. They were modeled with human features and given human hair and fiber beards. Their purpose is obscure; according to some accounts they were merely kept as relics. However, they were also used in ceremonies by men who distributed shell valuables. Some of them, in fact, have small wooden crossbars in the back that show signs of having been gripped by a wearer's teeth.

Collected 1880–81
Gift of Faith-dorian and Martin Wright, New York, to American Friends of the Israel Museum, in memory of Abraham Janoff

Mask (*lorr*, "skull")
New Britain, Gazelle Peninsula: Tolai
Late 19th – early 20th century
Human skull, clay, parinarium-nut paste,
paint, wood
Height 17.8 cm
B92.1593

This austere mask belongs to a type of which few examples exist, and whose function is uncertain. The others in a similar style share the same mop of fiber "hair," the arched eyebrows, sea-snail opercula eyes, triangular noses, and overall coat of white paint. The main difference is that some of these masks have firmly rounded chins. Most of them were collected, during a German expedition in 1875, in an area on the southwest coast of New Ireland.

It recalls with its thick hair the *tatanua* masks of northern New Ireland – an example of which is shown below (p. 292) – and with its stark white face the coloration of the famous *nalik* figures of the Uli rites of central New Ireland. It also bears some features in common with certain Tolai masks from the Duke of York Islands of north New Britain, inabited by emigrants from New Ireland. At the same time, the masks of this kind have an individuality that suggests they were specific to the small area in which they were found.

Formerly in the Museum für Völkerkunde, Leipzig
Gift of Faith-dorian and Martin Wright, New York, to American Friends of the Israel Museum, in memory of Abraham Janoff

Gunn, 1997

Mask
Southwestern New Ireland or
Duke of York Islands
Wood, paint, fiber, sea-snail opercula
Height 44 cm
B91.220

Throughout New Ireland, religious life is largely involved with rituals associated with death. In the northern part of the island, and in the islands nearby, where they go by the general name *malanggan*, these rituals are among the most spectacular of their kind in the whole Pacific area. Besides memorializing the dead, they are also manifestations of the relationships between clans and embodiments of the clans' power and prestige.

Preparations for *malanggan* celebrations begin shortly after the death, and may last for a considerable period. Gifts and feast foods that must be offered to the participants have to be assembled; but above all, the relatives of the deceased must commission from master sculptors a number of wood carvings also known as *malanggan*.

There are many different types of such carvings, from long friezes to individual human figures to compositions of groups in the round, including flying fish and birds. The *malanggan* carvings refer to clan spirits and their mythology. All of them boast fantastic complexity enhanced by attached openwork panels and a dazzling use of paint, in detailed red, yellow, black, and white patterns. They are finally exhibited at the funerary ceremonies, to the admiration of the attending crowd; having appeared once, they are usually destroyed.

This example is typical of the virtuoso openwork style of New Ireland carving. It relates to a type of *malanggan* called *kepong* (an ambiguous term that can apply to a whole range of objects) or *ges*, which – according to one of the many explanations of these works – are spirits of the wild living in trees. The *ges* head usually has a thin openwork plaque set at a right angle to the face. Like others, this *malanggan* was planted upright in the ground by the short post at the bottom. A form of mask with the same facial features is also called *ges* or *kepong*.

Gift of Faith-dorian and Martin Wright, New York, to American Friends of the Israel Museum, in memory of Abraham Janoff

Lincoln, 1987; *Gunn*, 1997

Funerary carving (*malanggan*)
New Ireland
Late 19th – early 20th century
Wood, paint
Height 136 cm
B85.0347

Among the array of *malanggan* carvings are masks, which also exist in many forms. Some share the same degree of elaboration as the funerary carvings, and are thus too heavy and fragile for dancing; these can only be put on display, or worn by stationary men. Others are actually worn by dancers, such as the *tatanua* masks. Like the other *malanggan*s, they apparently originated on the island of Tabar, off the northwest coast of New Ireland itself; over time, however, their use has spread into the central area of New Ireland. The wood faces of the masks are crowned with crests of fiber, modeling the hairstyle formerly worn by those in mourning. The masks do, in fact, represent individual dead men, and are called by their names.

Formerly in the Museum für Völkerkunde, Leipzig
Collected before 1914
Gift of Faith-dorian and Martin Wright, New York, to American Friends of the Israel Museum, in memory of Abraham Janoff

Lincoln, 1987; *Gunn*, 1997

Mask (*tatanua*)
New Ireland, northern area
Late 19th – early 20th century
Wood, paint, fiber, sea-snail opercula
Height 42 cm
B94.0418

While funeral rites in the north of New Ireland take the form of the *malanggan* celebrations with their complex wood carvings, in the central regions, the major cult objects were massive, single wooden figures (*nalik*) of seemingly hermaphroditic ancestors. They were displayed at the ceremonies called Uli.

In the southern area of New Ireland, where the people are allied to the Tolai of the New Britain coast, the cult objects are carved in chalk, like the sacred objects of the Inyet society. Unlike the Inyet carvings, but to some extent parallel to the *nalik*, they are exclusively figures of human beings, male and female. Made at the deaths of notable men and women, they were housed in miniature huts in secret enclosures in the forest; women were forbidden to see them.

In the terms of traditional ritual, these ancestral figures were supposed to be broken and abandoned after a certain period had elapsed. Clearly, this regulation was not always observed in the wake of Western contact, and subsequently commerce in the objects began in the late nineteenth century.

Gift of Faith-dorian and Martin Wright, New York, to American Friends of the Israel Museum, in memory of Abraham Janoff

Ancestral figure (*kulap*)
New Ireland, southern area: Patpatar
Late 19th – early 20th century
Chalk, paint
Height 42 cm
B94.0410

The islanders of the western Solomons built enormous canoes, carrying thirty men, which they used on head-hunting raids that continued up to the end of the nineteenth century. The raids were carried out to commemorate the launching of new canoes, marriages, and yam harvests – or simply in reprisal for other raids.

War canoes (*tomoko*) were constructed of sewn-together planks, and had slender uprights rising high from the prow and stern. The whole vessel was stained black, to which large white ovulum shells, attached from top to bottom of the front edges of the uprights, formed a vivid contrast.

At the bottom of the prow, just above the waterline, was fixed a small carving of a human torso known as the *musumusu* or *nguzunguzu*. Intended to protect the canoe's crew from *kesoko*, malevolent water spirits, they also symbolized the raid's purpose: the capture of human heads.

As in this example, most of the *musumusu* or *nguzunguzu* are also stained black, with white shell inlays simulating face-paint designs, and huge earlobes representing ear ornaments. The hands usually hold small human heads, anticipating the result of the raid. The large, curved projections from the top of the head, found mainly on New Georgia *nguzunguzu*, resemble the Solomon Islands convention for the wings of the seagoing frigate bird, as shown on other objects such as shell ornaments. The projections probably have the same significance here.

Gift of the Faith-dorian and Martin Wright Family, New York, to American Friends of the Israel Museum

Waite, 1983

Canoe prow figure (*musumusu* or
nguzunguzu)
Western Solomon Islands,
New Georgia group, Roviana
Late 19th – early 20th century
Wood, paint, shell
Height 33 cm
B00.0635

The warriors of the southeastern Solomon Islands used a unique defensive weapon in their fights: ostensibly a long, thin club with a flat curved blade, it is actually a light shield carried in the left hand to deflect spears. A thin ridge running along the middle of the curved upper part terminates in a snake's head, probably a symbol of aggression. The little figure close to the butt end is rendered in the typical chunky southern Solomons style, but its head is very reminiscent of the carved heads of *musumusu* guardian spirits that were attached to the prows of war canoes in the Solomon Islands to the north. Perhaps the figure was similarly intended to protect its owner. The use of "ugi" in the name seems to indicate that this type of shield originated on Ugi Island.

Gift of Faith-dorian and Martin Wright, New York, to American Friends of the Israel Museum, in memory of Abraham Janoff

Mead, 1973

Shield (*roromaraugi*)
Solomon Islands, southeast area,
Santa Ana or San Cristobal Islands
Late 19th – early 20th century
Wood
Height 140 cm
346.85

The men of Vanuatu (formerly, the New Hebrides) are members of a type of organization which, although called by several different names across the islands of the group, follows the same structure everywhere. The organization, or "society," consists of a hierarchy of grades of ascending prestige, each with its attendant title and privileges. Every man begins in the lowest of the grades; throughout his life, he attempts to work his way up to the highest.

Success involves his ability to organize and pay for the great rituals of passage from grade to grade, including the feasting and sacrifices that accompany them. The rituals demand the slaughter of numbers of boars specially bred to grow spiral tusks (the more curves, the more valuable the animal). The rise in grade is marked by the carving of a figure in the type prescribed for that grade. According to the grade, the figures are carved in wood or the fibrous trunk of a tree fern, and painted with the style of body decoration appropriate to the grade's members.

Gift of Faith-dorian and Martin Wright, New York, to American Friends of the Israel Museum, in memory of Abraham Janoff

Grade society figure
Vanuatu, Ambrym Island
Late 19th – early 20th century
Fernwood, paint
Height 200 cm
146.84

Temes Nevimbur ("Nevimbur ghosts") are marionettes, representing either spirit beings or actual persons, that play several different ritual roles in south Malakula. It is said, in fact, that they were formerly made by the hundreds. Modeled around a staff, they may be half-figures with extended arms (as here) or no more than heads.

The *temes Nevimbur* owe their name to their appearance in the initiations of a secret men's society called Nevimbur. During these rites, three life-sized figures were set up in front of a fence; they represented Mansip, a mythical hero, and his two wives. The *temes*, as their children, were manipulated by men behind the fence to make them bob up and down and wave their arms as though dancing. The performance ended with the mock "killing," by the leader of the rite, of the three main figures, whose "blood" was represented by a cascade of red plant juice. The *temes* were also "killed" by smashing their heads.

Temes were also presented at the ceremonies inaugurating a *rambaramp*, the memorial figure for a deceased great man that was carved in fernwood, richly decorated with his grade ornaments and paint designs, and topped with his skull after it had been modeled and painted to simulate his features. Here the *temes*, planted in the ground, stood for the man's children.

Gift of Vivien and Edward M. Merrin, New York, to American Friends of the Israel Museum

Deacon, 1970

Figure (*temes Nevimbur*)
Vanuatu, southern Malakula Island:
Mbotgote
Late 19th – early 20th century
Vegetable materials, pig tusks,
feathers, paint
Height 116 cm
659.76

The houses of chiefs in New Caledonia were built in conical form, with peaks that rose up to twenty meters high. They were sacred spaces, equivalent to the ceremonial houses of other parts of Melanesia and New Guinea. Inside and out, they were decorated with a wealth of sculptures, including carved posts, doorjambs, lintels, sills, and ancestral figures from the various clans making up the community. Above all, the peak of the building was crowned with a large finial figure.

The finials were carved from a species of tree believed to house the souls of important men of the past. The several local styles differed in details, but shared basic characteristics. All are strongly silhouetted, shallow objects, with a low-relief face in the central part that has geometric elements, often in openwork, above and below it; seemingly abstract, these elements actually represent parts of the body. A long, thin extension below is used to fasten the finial to the central pole of the house; another, rising above the face, is embellished with marine shells. The display of these highly prized objects was a statement of wealth.

Symbolically, the central pole of the house stood for the living chief – and the finial, for a deceased one. Upon the death of a chief, his maternal relatives would enter the village "to reclaim their blood"; among other things, they would claim and carry off the finial. The condition of this one attests to its age.

Gift of Faith-dorian and Martin Wright, New York, to American Friends of the Israel Museum, in memory of Abraham Janoff

Boulay, 1990a; *Guiart*, 1953

Roof finial
New Caledonia: Kanak
Late 19th – early 20th century
Wood, shell
Height 93 cm
555.82

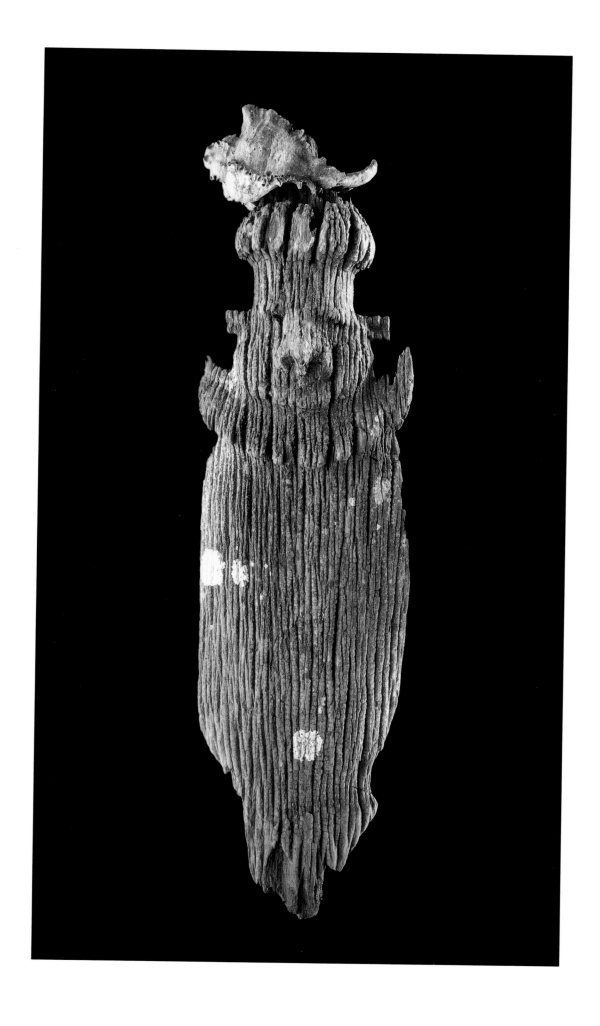

A Kanak chief was selected by a council of elders, and then began a course of training for his station. The elders saw to the cultivation of his physical and spiritual well-being, including protecting him with magic spells and feeding him with the flesh of human enemies, through which he assimilated the powers of their ancestors. In due course, he himself gained the supernatural status of an ancestor, with complete power over the land and his people.

Chiefs were presented with three objects of regalia: a carving of a bird, the finial of the great house, and a mask. The masks of New Caledonia were said, in mythology, to have arisen from the water, as was believed of other sacred objects in Melanesia; thus, one of their numerous functions was to embody water-spirits. The chief wore his mask in dances, during which he also carried a spear, in his right hand, and a club whose head resembled a bird's beak, in his left.

Gift of Faith-dorian and Martin Wright, New York, to American Friends of the Israel Museum, in memory of Abraham Janoff

Boulay, 1990b; *Guiart*, 1966

Mask
New Caledonia: Kanak
Late 19th – early 20th century
Wood, paint, feathers, human hair
Height 120 cm
B94.0408

Micronesia

Figural sculpture was rarely made in Micronesia apart from in the Caroline Islands, which yielded architectural pieces from the Belau (Palau) islands group, and a small number of statues of divinities from Nukuoro, an atoll. The figure shown here, attributed to the Tuvalu archipelago, is one of a very small number known in this style. A stylistically similar female figure, dating from before 1895, is said to hail from Nauru, considerably north of Tuvalu. The style also relates to certain figures from the Fiji Islands south of Tuvalu, suggesting that the ancestors of the islanders may well have been immigrant Polynesians.

If their sculpture is rare, Micronesians excelled in the crafts of weaving and plaiting plant fibers, from which they produced mats, small boxes, and ornaments of great elegance. Micronesian body ornaments ingeniously incorporated other natural materials from animal and sea life.

Kaniet is one of a group of small islands near the Admiralty Islands scantily inhabited by peripheral Micronesian populations. The relatively few carved works from Kaniet are characterized by bearded faces, and by notching along their edges, a feature also found in early Polynesian sculpture.

Head circlet: Formerly in the Herz Jesu Hiltruper Mission, Hiltrup bei Munster
All objects: Gifts of Faith-dorian and Martin Wright, New York, to American Friends of the Israel Museum,
in memory of Abraham Janoff

Kaniet: *Bourgoin*, 1997

Figure
Tuvalu (formerly Ellice Islands)
Late 19th – early 20th century
Wood, shell
Height 30 cm
B94.0409

Head circlet
Nauru
Late 19th – early 20th century
Plant stems, feathers, crab shell,
shark teeth
Diameter 9 cm
B98.0024

Man's comb
Northwestern Islands, Kaniet Island
Late 19th – early 20th century
Wood
Height 18 cm
351.85

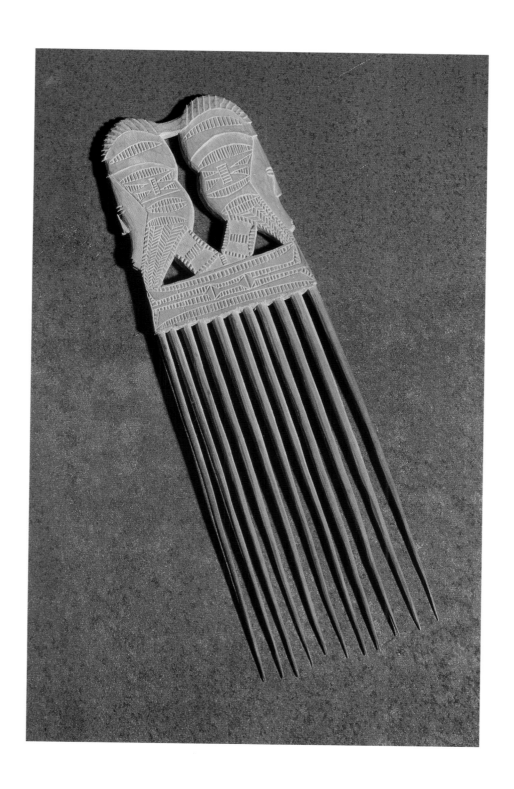

Polynesia

Easter Island – or Rapa Nui, its indigenous name – in the far eastern Pacific Ocean is not only tiny (no more than 166 square kilometers) but also one of the most isolated places in the world. Formed from the detritus of three extinct volcanoes, Easter Island is 3,600 kilometers from the coast of South America. This far-flung frontier was nevertheless discovered and settled by Polynesians about 1,400 years ago. There they developed a culture, including an art style, which proved a distinctive variation on that of the rest of Polynesia. Through wars and misuse of natural resources, the islanders degraded their environment irreparably, and consequently much of their culture was in decline prior to the arrival of Westerners.

The enormous stone colossi of Easter Island, whose creation must have consumed a great deal of the available manpower, are unparalleled in the Pacific and famous worldwide. At the same time, the islanders were accomplished wood-carvers, their best-known works being figures of skeletal males and flat, frontally posed females. Besides these, there exists a large group of small carvings showing highly eccentric human images, some cut from naturally distorted pieces of wood, as in this case. These figures have great intensity, although their function and the intentions of the artists who made them are not certainly known. Some of the figures are pierced at the back of the neck, presumably for the purpose of suspending them, suggesting that they might have been amulets.

Gift of Faith-dorian and Martin Wright, New York, to American Friends of the Israel Museum, in memory of Karen Hess

Heyerdahl, 1975; Orliac and Orliac, 1995

Figure
Easter Island
18th century
Wood
Height 16 cm
B95.0089

Clubs were the favored weapons of the Polynesians. Easter Island clubs, while probably just as deadly as any others, were the simplest in form to be found in Polynesia. They are long, plain staffs, their upper ends carved with Janus faces (in the usual convention of the art) featuring high cheekbones, striated hair, and small round eyes of obsidian and bird bone.

The Fijians made at least a dozen different major types of clubs, each with several named variants. Club-makers were specialized craftsmen who were rewarded with feasts and valuables; the engraved designs of the shafts and heads were executed separately by other specialists. Beyond their use in fighting, clubs were also carried in dancing, while enormous clubs of impractical size were made as spectacular gifts or for ritual purposes.

Totokia clubs were sometimes called "kingfisher beaks," since their point was used to "peck" a hole in the enemy's skull. The heavy weight of the head behind the point meant that the man who wielded it could administer a short jab, rather than needing a wide swing. This was particularly advantageous in fighting at close quarters.

Central Polynesians often used a double-ended weapon combining a club blade and a sharpened point, as did the Maori of New Zealand. By a process of elaboration, the Maori developed the point into a human head with an aggressive, protruding tongue. *Taiaha* were also used as staffs by chiefs, decorated with red feathers (much prized by nearly all Polynesians) as a mark of prestige.

Easter Island club: Gift of Mr. and Mrs. Samuel Dubiner, Ramat Gan

Maori club: Gift of Faith-dorian and Martin Wright, New York, to American Friends of the Israel Museum, in memory of Abraham Janoff

Fiji club: Gift of Jacob Hector, New York, to American Friends of the Israel Museum

Easter Island: *Heyerdahl*, 1975; Maori: Buck, 1982; Fiji: *Clunie*, 1977

Club (*u'a*)
Easter Island
Late 19th – early 20th century
Wood, bird bone, obsidian
Length 87 cm
1099.2.56

Spear club (*taiaha*)
New Zealand: Maori
Late 19th – early 20th century
Wood, fur, shell, feathers
Length 147 cm
1166.78

Club (*totokia* type)
Fiji
Late 19th – early 20th century
Wood
Length 73 cm
552.2.55

This model of a *bure kalou* ("house spirit," house of the spirit) replicates in miniature the form and proportions of the large temples that were to be seen in most Fijian towns and villages. A building of this kind stood in a fenced enclosure on top of an earth platform about six meters high, faced with stone blocks. The *bure* itself was rectangular, with walls of planking sometimes carved with relief figures. The pitched thatch roof rose about three times the height of the walls to a ridgepole that projected at either end; the pole was decorated with strings of sacred white ovulum shells.

The main feature of the temple's interior was a length of white bark-cloth hanging from the ceiling down to the floor. The cloth screened one of the corner posts, thus creating a sacred space in front of which sat the presiding priest. Otherwise, the interior was usually quite bare, except for a few offerings of whale teeth, headrests, and other minor objects. The model temples, considered the temporary abodes of gods, were kept behind the screen.

As the intermediary between gods and men, the priest was asked to intercede for aid in critical undertakings, and for predictions of their outcomes. On appeals from the priest, the god descended the bark-cloth "path" and entered into him. In this state of possession, the priest delivered the god's reply. Some priests questioned the god through the temple models (which may have contained small images of the deity) and received answers through them.

Formerly in the Hofrat Dr. E. Sieglin Collection
Gift of Faith-dorian and Martin Wright, New York, to American Friends of the Israel Museum, in memory of Abraham Janoff

Clunie, 1986

Model temple (*bure kalou*)
Fiji
Late 19th – early 20th century
Wood, sennit (coconut fiber cord),
shells
Height 81.9 cm
B92.1592

Many of the eastern island groups of Polynesia – the Society Islands, Hawai'i, the Cook Islands, and New Zealand – practiced the skill or sport of stilt-walking, often as a children's game. In the Marquesas Islands, boys began to practice stilt-walking at an early age. There, however, it was also a part of ritual life, and women were barred from engaging in it. During festivals in honor of the dead, particularly important priests, men took part in competitive races on stilts. Part of the object was to topple one's opponents during the course of the race.

Marquesan stilts were unique in their elaborate decoration. The slender wooden shafts were incised with low-relief patterns, and the steps, or footrests, were separate lashed-on carvings in the round. There are many minor variations in the design of these stilt steps, but the main feature is always at least one human figure who appears to support the flange on which the foot was placed. Called *tiki*, they follow the standardized Marquesan representation of the human form, featuring large heads, faces with enormous round eyes, and small, stocky bodies. The striations engraved on the figures are simplified versions of the elaborate tattooing that often covered the entire body of a Marquesan man.

Gift of Mr. and Mrs. Samuel Dubiner, Ramat Gan

Handy, 1938; *von den Steinen*, 1969 [1925]

Stilt step (*tapuvahe*)
Marquesas Islands
Late 19th – early 20th century
Wood
Height 40 cm
1072.2.56

The Hawai'ians became renowned, shortly after they were first contacted by Europeans in 1779, for the magnificence of their featherwork, which included huge cloaks and capes, helmets, and feathered god-images. Tremendous labor and numbers of birds were involved; indeed, some 500,00 feathers could be used in a single cloak. Naturally, such masterpieces were the prerogatives of the very highest chiefs. Aristocratic women wore small bands of feathers (*lei*) as necklaces or hair ornaments. While the red feathers were revered – red being a sacred color throughout Polynesia – yellow was often preferred, and ultimately became Hawai'i's national color.

Hook-like pendants (perhaps based on actual fishhooks) have an ancient history in Polynesia, where they were widespread; the earliest-known Hawai'ian example is about 1,000 years old. These were also high-status ornaments, as they still are today, and were often used as ceremonial gifts.

The preferred material for these hooks was whale ivory, but owing to its scarcity before European contact, the pendants were often made of shell, stone, coral, and even lowly wood if all else failed; originally, they were often only a few centimeters long. With the rise of the whaling industry in the nineteenth century, in which many Polynesians partook as crew members, whale teeth and walrus tusks became readily available, and the size of the pendants tripled. The pendants were hung by a perforation at the top of the hook, on thick bundles of string braided from human hair. In some cases, up to 300 meters of it were used.

The symbolism of the *lei niho palaoa* was probably quite complex. The curved section is said to be a container for its owner's *mana* (spiritual power) or the jaw of a god, thus referring to the chiefly owner's divine ancestry.

Gifts of the Faith-dorian and Martin Wright Family, New York, to American Friends of the Israel Museum

Buck, 1964

Feather ornament (*lei*)
Hawai'i
19th century
Feathers on band
Length 40 cm
B96.026

Pendant (*lei niho palaoa*)
Hawai'i
19th century
Ivory, human hair, cord
Length 30 cm
B96.027

The Maori of New Zealand were the greatest canoe builders of the Pacific. Their enormous sailing canoes, constructed from huge, hollowed-out tree trunks with sides built up with planking, could carry up to sixty men on war or trading expeditions. They were outfitted with large, elaborate carved prows and stern posts trimmed with bunches and streamers of feathers.

Other canoe accessories were also carved and painted, including paddles and bailers. This example of a bailer shows the characteristic head of an enigmatic mythological creature called *manaia* on the tip of the handle, and a stylized face at the handle's juncture with the bowl. Some of these bailers were heirlooms known by the names of ancestors.

Gift of Faith-dorian and Martin Wright, New York, to American Friends of the Israel Museum, in memory of Abraham Janoff

Best, 1976

Canoe bailer (*tiheru*)
New Zealand: Maori
Late 19th – early 20th century
Wood
Height 13 cm
1164.78

The central building of each Maori community was – and still is – a meeting house known as *whare whakairo* ("carved house"). As part of a renaissance of Maori culture that has been taking place over the last few decades, a large number of new houses have been built and invested with as great symbolic and social significance as ever before.

The meeting house symbolizes the founding ancestor of each group, and is intended to constitute a re-creation of his body. The ridgepole is his spine; a mask over the front gable is his face; bargeboards bordering the gable are his arms; and the rafters connote his ribs. Metaphorically, the ancestor gathers his descendants within him when they enter the house.

From early times, this imagery was expressed in the decoration of the house, inside and out. This distinctive embellishment achieved its highest point about the mid-nineteenth century. The interior of the house was lined with broad wood panels, carved in relief, alternating with panels of reeds plaited into symbolic abstract patterns. Each of the wood panels bore a frontally posed figure of a tribal ancestor. In this example, an ancestral figure is shown flanked on either side with one of the bird-like spirits called *manaia*. The ancestor's tongue is out-thrust, an aggressive gesture that recurs often in Maori visual art and in the famous *haka* war dances. The figure's face is covered with the tattooed designs of a high-status chief. The objects in his hands are a form of *manaia* known as *torea*, or "skinny"; the word also refers to the oystercatcher and stilt birds.

An almost identical panel (but showing a female ancestor), now in the Auckland Institute and Museum, was carved in 1860 for an Arawa chief by the artist Wero of the Ngati Tarawhai tribe. The resemblance suggests that the panel shown here was made by the same sculptor.

Gift of Lawrence, Dennis, Frank, and John Natan, Auckland, New Zealand

Mead, ed., 1984; *Phillips,* 1952; Wero and *torea: Dr. Roger Neich (personal communication)*

Wall panel (*poupou*)
New Zealand: Maori,
Te Arawa tribal area
Mid-19th century
Wood, paint
Height 240 cm
75.40.91

Bibliography

Africa

Bandelier, Georges. *Daily Life in the Kingdom of the Kongo from the Sixteenth to the Eighteenth Century.* New York: Pantheon Books, 1968.

Barbier, Jean Paul, ed. *Art of Côte d'Ivoire from the Collection of the Barbier-Mueller Museum.* 2 vols. Geneva: The Barbier-Mueller Museum, 1993.

Bastin, M.-L. "L'art d'un peuple d'Angola: Lwena." *African Arts* 2, no. 3 (1969): 46–53, 77–80.

Biebuyck, Daniel P. "Bembe Art." *African Arts* 5, no. 3 (1972): 12–19, 75–84.

——. *Lega Culture: Art, Initiation, and Moral Philosophy among a Central African People.* Berkeley: University of California Press, 1973.

——. *The Arts of Zaire.* 2 vols. Berkeley, Los Angeles, and London: University of California Press, 1986.

Blakely, T. D., and P. A. B. Blakely. "So'o Masks and Hemba Funerary Festival." *African Arts* 21, no. 1 (1987): 30–37, 84–86.

Blier, Susan P. *Royal Art of Africa: The Majesty of Form.* London: Lawrence King, 1998.

Bochet, Gilbert. "The Poro of the Senufo." In Barbier, ed., 1: 54–85, 1993.

Boone, Sylvia Ardyn. *Radiance from the Waters: Ideals of Feminine Beauty in Mende Art.* New Haven: Yale University Press, 1986.

Bourgeois, Arthur. *Art of the Yaka and Suku.* Meudon: Alain et Françoise Chaffin, 1984.

Boyer, Alain-Michel. "Art of the Baule." In Barbier, ed., 1: 302–367, 1993.

Bravmann, Rene A. *Islam and Tribal Art in West Africa. African Studies series 11.* London: Cambridge University Press, 1974.

Cole, Herbert M., and Chike C. Aniakor. *Igbo Arts: Community and Cosmos.* Los Angeles: Museum of Cultural History, University of California, 1977.

Cornet, Joseph. *Art of Africa: Treasures from the Congo.* London: Phaidon Press, 1971.

——. *Art royal kuba.* Milan: Sipiel, 1982.

De Grunne, Bernard. *The Birth of Art in Black Africa: Nok Statuary in Nigeria.* Paris: Adam Biro, 1988.

Dells, Arraign. "The Guro." In Barbier, ed., 1: 234–245, 1993.

Drawl, Henry John, and John Pemberton III, with Rowland Abiodun. *Yoruba: Nine Centuries of African Art and Thought.* New York: The Center for African Art, 1989.

Eyo, Ekpo, and Frank Willett. *Treasures of Ancient Nigeria.* New York: Alfred A. Knopf; the Detroit Institute of Arts, 1980.

Ezra, Kate. *The Art of the Dogon: Selections from the Lester Wunderman Collection.* New York: The Metropolitan Museum of Art; Harry N. Abrams, 1988.

——. *Royal Art of Benin: The Perls Collection in the Metropolitan Museum of Art.* New York: The Metropolitan Museum of Art; Harry N. Abrams, 1992.

Felix, Marc L. *Kipinga: Throwing-blades of Africa.* Munich: Verlag Fred Jahn, 1991.

Fischer, Eberhard, and Hans Himmelheber. *Die Kunst der Dan.* Zurich: Museum Rietberg, 1976.

Fischer, Eberhard, and Lorenz Homberger. *Die Kunst der Guro, Elfenbeinküste.* Zürich: Museum Rietberg, 1985.

Gabus, Jean. *Au Sahara. Arts et symboles.* Neuchatel: À La Baconnière, 1958.

Glaze, Anita. *Art and Death in a Senufo Village.* Bloomington: Indiana University Press, 1981.

Hersak, Dunja. *Songye Masks and Figure Sculptures.* London: Ethnographica, 1986.

Huet, J. C. "The Togu Na of Tenyu Ireli." *African Arts* 21, no. 4 (1988): 31–36, 91.

Imperato, Pascal. "Sogoni koun." *African Arts* 14, no. 2 (1981): 38–47.

Jansen, G., and J. G. Gauthier. *Ancient Art of the Northern Cameroons: Sao and Fali.* Oosterhout: Anthropological Publications, 1973.

Kerchache, J., J.-L. Paudrat, and L. Stephan. *L'art africain.* Paris: Citadelles/Mazenod, 1988.

Kreamer, C. M. "Moba Shrine Figures." *African Arts* 20, no. 2 (1987): 52–55, 82–84.

Lebeuf, Jean-Paul, and Annie Lebeuf. *Les arts des Sao. Cameroun, Tchad, Nigeria.* Paris: Éditions du Chêne, 1977.

Lewis-Williams, D. "The San Artistic Achievement." *African Arts* 18, no. 3 (1985): 54–59, 100.

Loughran, Kristyne. *Art from the Forge.* Washington, D.C.: National Museum of African Art, 1995.

Mack, John. *Madagascar: Island of the Ancestors.* London: The British Museum, 1986.

McNaughton, P. R. "Is There History in Horizontal Masks? A Preliminary Response to the Dilemma of Form." *African Arts* 24, no. 2 (1991): 40–53, 88–89.

Meyer, Piet. *Kunst und Religion der Lobi (West Africa).* Zurich: Museum Rietburg, 1981.

Neyt, François. *Le grand statuaire hemba du Zaire.* Louvain-la-Neuve: Institut supérieure d'archéologie et d'histoire d'art, 1977.

Nicklin, K. "Kuyu Sculpture at the Powell-Cotton Museum." *African Arts* 17, no. 1 (1983): 55–59, 88.

Northern, Tamara. *The Sign of the Leopard: Beaded Art of Cameroon.* Storrs: University of Connecticut, 1975.

Perrois, Louis. *Ancestral Art of Gabon from the Collection of the Barbier-Mueller Museum.* Geneva: Barbier-Mueller Museum, 1986.

Perrois, Louis, and Marta Sierra Delage. *The Art of Equatorial Guinea: The Fang Tribes.* Barcelona: Fundacion Folch, Ediciones Poligrafa, 1991.

Phillips, Tom, ed. *Africa: The Art of a Continent.* London: The Royal Academy of Arts and Prestel-Verlag, 1988.

Prussin, Labelle, *African Nomadic Architecture: Space, Place, and Gender.* Washington, D.C.: Smithsonian Institution Press, The National Museum of African Art, 1995.

Ravenhill, Philip L. "Baule Statuary Art, Meaning and Modernization." *Special Issue on Baule Aesthetics. Working Papers in the Traditional Arts 5 & 6.* Philadelphia: Institute for the Study of Human Issues, 1980.

Roberts, Mary Nooter, and Alan F. Roberts, eds. *Memory: Luba Art and the Making of History.* Munich: Prestel; New York: The Museum for African Art, 1996.

Roy, Christopher. *Art of the Upper Volta Rivers.* Meudon: Alain et Françoise Chaffin, 1987.

Scheinberg, Alfred. *Art of the Igbo, Ibibio, Ogoni.* New York: Endicott-Guthan Gallery, 1975.

Schildkrout, Enid, and C. A. Keim. *African Reflections: Art from Northeastern Zaire.* Seattle: University of Washington; American Museum of Natural History, 1990.

Schmalenbach, Werner. *African Art from the Barbier-Mueller Collection.* New York: Prestel-Verlag, 1988.

Sieber, Roy. "Art and History in Ghana." In Forge, ed., 1973: 70–96.

Sieber, Roy, and Tony Vevers. *Interaction: The Art Styles of the Benue River Valley and East Nigeria.* Lafayette: Purdue University, 1974.

Sousberghe, L. de. *L'art pende*, Beaux-Arts, 9, fasc. 2, 1958.

Talbot, P. Amaury. *Life in Southern Nigeria: The Magic, Beliefs and Customs of the Ibibio Tribe.* London: Macmillan & Co., 1923.

Thompson, Robert Farris. *African Art in Motion: Icon and Act.* Berkeley and Los Angeles: University of California Press, 1974. Vansina, Jan. *The Children of Woot: A History of the Kuba Peoples.* Dawson: University of Wisconsin Press, 1976.

Verswijver, Gustaaf, et al., eds. *The Tervuren Museum: Masterpieces from Central Africa.* Munich and New York: Prestel, 1996.

Vogel, Susan, ed. *For Spirits and Kings: African Art from the Paul and Ruth Tishman Collection.* New York: The Metropolitan Museum of Art, 1981.

Vogel, Susan M. "Beauty in the Eyes of the Baule: Aesthetics and Cultural Values." *Special Issue on Baule Aesthetics. Working Papers in the Traditional Arts 5 & 6.* Philadelphia: Institute for the Study of Human Issues, 1980.

——. *Baule – African Art, Western Eyes.* New Haven and London: Yale University Press, 1997.

Willett, Frank. *Ife in the History of West African Sculpture.* New York: McGraw-Hill Book Company, 1961.

Wolfe, Ernie. *An Introduction to the Arts of Kenya.* Washington, D.C.: National Museum of African Art, 1979.

Oceania

Barbier, Jean Paul, and Douglas Newton, eds. *Islands and Ancestors: Indigenous Styles of Southeast Asia.* New York: Prestel-Verlag, 1988.

Beran, Harry, and Anthony J. P. Meyer. *Le pays Massim. Papua-Nouvelle Guinée.* Paris: Galerie Meyer, 1987.

Best, Elsdon. *The Maori Canoe. Dominion Museum bulletin no. 7.* Wellington: Government Printer, 1976 (first printing 1925).

Bodrogi, Tibor. *Art in North-east Guinea.* Budapest: Hungarian Academy of Sciences, 1961.

Bonnemaison, Joel, Kirk Huffman, Christian Kaufmann, and Darrell Tryon. *Art of Vanuatu.* Honolulu: University of Hawai'i Press, 1996.

Boulay, Roger. *La maison kanak.* Paris: Édition de l'Orstom, 1990.

——. *De jade et de nacre. Patrimoine artistique kanak.* Paris: Réunion des musées nationaux, 1990.

Bougoin, Philippe. "The Forgotten Islands of the Bismarck Archipelago: The Hermits and Kaniets." *The World of Tribal Arts* 4, no. 1 (1997): 64–79.

——. "War Charms of the Admiralty Islands." *The World of Tribal Arts* 5, no. 2 (1998): 84–95.

Bowden, Ross. *Yena: Art and Ceremony in a Sepik Society. Monograph 3.* University of Oxford: Pitt Rivers Museum, 1983.

Buck, Peter H. (Te Rangi Hiroa). *Arts and Crafts of Hawaii. Special publication 45.* Honolulu: Bernice P. Bishop Museum Press, 1964.

——. *The Coming of the Maori.* Wellington: Whitcoulls Ltd., 1982 (first printing 1949).

Casino, E. S., Fr. G. Casal, R. T. Jose, Jr., G. R. Ellis, and W. G. Solheim III. *The People and Art of the Philippines.* Los Angeles: Museum of Cultural History, University of California, 1981.

Casino, Eric S. "Arts and Peoples of the Southern Philippines." In Casino et al.: 123–181, 1981.

Clunie, Fergus. *Fijian Weapons & Warfare. Bulletin of the Fiji Museum no. 2.* Suva: Fiji Museum, 1977.

——. *Yalo I Viti: Shades of Fiji. Fiji Museum catalogue.* Suva: Fiji Museum, 1986.

Corbin, George. "The Art of the Baining: New Britain," in S. M. Mead, ed.: 159–179, 1979.

Deacon, A. B. *Malekula: A Vanishing People in the New Hebrides.* London: George Routledge, 1970 (first printing 1934).

Dournes, Jacques. "Autochthonous Peoples of Central Vietnam," in Barbier and Newton, eds.: 24–33, 1988.

Duarte, Jorge Barros. "Atauro: One of the Sunda Islands." *Tribal Art (Barbier-Mueller Museum Bulletin)* 1 (1990): 17–32.

Ellis, George R. "Arts and Peoples of the Northern Philippines." In Casino et al.: 183–263, 1981.

Forge, Anthony. "Art and Environment in the Sepik. The Curl Lecture 1965." *Proceedings of the Royal Anthropological Institute of Great Britain and Ireland 1965*: 23–31.

——. "Style and Meaning in Sepik Art." In Forge, ed.: 169–192, 1973.

Forge, Anthony, ed. *Primitive Art & Society.* London, New York: Oxford University Press, 1973.

Greub, Suzanne, ed. *Art of Northwest New Guinea from Geelvink Bay, Humboldt Bay, and Lake Sentani.* New York: Rizzoli, 1992.

Guiart, Jean. *L'art authochtone de Nouvelle Calédonie.* Nouméa: Imprimeries Réunies de Nouméa, 1953.

——. *Mythologie du masque en Nouvelle Calédonie. Publication no. 18.* Paris: Société des Océanistes, 1966.

Gunn, Michael. *Ritual Arts of Oceania: New Ireland in the Collections of the Musée Barbier-Mueller*. Milan: Skira Editore, 1997.

Haberland, Eike. *The Caves of Karawari*. New York: D'Arcy Galleries, 1968.

Haberland, Eike, and Siegfried Seyfarth. *Die Yimar am Oberen Korowori (Neuguinea)*. Wiesbaden: Franz Steiner Verlag, 1974.

Handy, Willowdean C. *L'art des îles Marquises*. Paris: Éditions d'Art et d'Histoire, 1938.

Hauser-Schäublin, Brigitta. *Kulthäuser in Nordneuguinea*. Abhandlungen und Berichte des Staatlichen Museums für Völkerkunde Dresden. Forschungsstelle. Band 43. Monographien 7. Berlin: Akademie-Verlag, 1989.

Heyerdahl, Thor. *The Art of Easter Island*. New York: Doubleday & Company, 1975.

Kaeppler, Adrienne, Christian Kaufmann, and Douglas Newton. *Oceanic Art*. New York: Harry N. Abrams, 1997.

Kaufmann, Christian. "Ethnographische Notizen zur Basler Korewori-Sammlung." *Verhandlungen der Naturforschenden Gesellschaft in Basel* 84 (1974): 711–724.

Kooijman, Simon. *The Art of Lake Sentani*. New York: The Museum of Primitive Art, 1959.

Kooijman, Simon, and Jac. Hoogerbrugge. "Art of Wakde-Yamna Area, Humboldt Bay, and Lake Sentani." In Greub, ed.: 57–125, 1992.

Lincoln, Louise, ed. *Assemblage of Spirits: Idea and Image in New Ireland*. New York: George Braziller and the Minneapolis Institute of Arts, 1987.

Lutkehaus, Nancy, Christian Kaufmann, William E. Mitchell, Douglas Newton, Lita Osmunden, and Meinhard Schuster, eds. *Sepik Heritage: Tradition and Change in New Guinea*. Durham, N.C.: Carolina Academic Press, 1990.

May, Patricia, and Margaret Tuckson. *The Traditional Pottery of Papua New Guinea*. Sydney: Bay Books, 1982.

Mead, S. M. *Material Culture and Art in the Star Harbour Region, Eastern Solomon Islands. Ethnography monograph 1.* Toronto: Royal Ontario Museum, 1973.

Mead, S. M., ed. *Exploring the Visual Art of Oceania: Australia, Melanesia, Micronesia, and Polynesia*. Honolulu: University of Hawai'i Press, 1979.

——. *Te Maori: Maori Art from New Zealand Collections*. New York: The Museum of Primitive Art, 1975.

Newton, Douglas, ed. *Arts of the South Seas*. London, Munich, and New York: Prestel-Verlag, 1999.

Ohnemus, Sylvia. *An Ethnology of the Admiralty Islanders. The Alfred Buhler Collection, in the Museum für Kulturen, Basel*. Honolulu: Crawford Publishing House; University of Hawai'i Press, 1998.

Orliac, C., and M. Orliac. *Bois sculptés de l'île de Pâques*. Marseilles: Éditions Parenthèses, 1995.

Phillips, W. J. *Maori Houses and Food Stores. Dominion Museum monograph no. 8.* Wellington: Government Printer, 1952.

Schmitz, C. A. *Oceanic Art: Man, Myth and Image in the South Seas*. New York: Harry N. Abrams, 1969.

Schuster, Meinhard. "Die Maler vom May River." *Palette* 33 (1969): 1–19.

Scoditti, Giancarlo M. G. *Kitawa: A Linguistic and Aesthetic Analysis of Visual Art in Melanesia*. Berlin and New York: Mouton de Gruyter, 1990.

Smidt, Dirk A. M., ed. *Asmat Art: Woodcarvings of Southwest New Guinea*. Leiden: Periplus Editions; Rijksmuseum voor Volkenkunde, 1993.

Taylor, Paul Michael, and Lorraine V. Aragon. *Beyond the Java Sea: Art of Indonesia's Outer Islands*. New York: The National Museum of Natural History, Harry N. Abrams, 1990.

Van Baaren, Theodore P. "Art of Geelvink Bay," in Greub, ed.: 17–55, 1992.

Von den Stienen, Karl. *Die Marquesaner und ihre Kunst*. 3 vols. New York: Hacker, 1969 (first printing 1925).

Waite, Deborah. *Art of the Solomon Islands from the Collection of the Barbier-Mueller Museum*. Geneva: Musée Barbier-Mueller, 1983.